Study Guide

to accompany

Carson • Lapsansky-Werner • Nash

AFRICAN AMERICAN LIVES

The Struggle for Freedom

Volume II

Abel A. Bartley

Clemson University

PEARSON

Longman

New York Boston San Francisco
London Toronto Sydney Tokyo Singapore Madrid
Mexico City Munich Paris Cape Town Hong Kong Montreal

Study Guide to accompany *African American Lives: The Struggle for Freedom, Volume II*

Copyright ©2006 Pearson Education, Inc.

ISBN: 0-321-33781-6

1 2 3 4 5 6 7 8 9 10– OPM –08 07 06 05

TABLE OF CONTENTS

Chapter 11 *Post-Civil War Reconstruction: A New National Era*   1

Chapter 12 *The Post-Reconstruction Era*   13

Chapter 13 Colored *Becomes* Negro *in the Progressive Era*   21

Chapter 14 *The Making of a* New Negro*: World War I to the Great Depression*   31

Chapter 15 *The New Politics of the Great Depression*   41

Chapter 16 *Fighting Fascism Abroad and Racism at Home*   51

Chapter 17 *Emergence of a Mass Movement Against Jim Crow*   61

Chapter 18 *Marching Toward Freedom, 1960-1969*   71

Chapter 19 *Resistance, Repression, and Retrenchment, 1967-1978*   81

Chapter 20 *The Search for New Directions During a Conservative Era, 1979-1991*   91

Chapter 21 *Continuing Struggles Over Rights and Identity, 1992-Present*   101

CHAPTER 11 *Post-Civil War Reconstruction: A New National Era*

CHAPTER SUMMARY

Opening Vignette: Emanuel Fortune Testifies Before Congress

In 1871, Florida Republican Emanuel Fortune told a congressional committee that despite constitutional guarantees, threats and violence prevented black southerners from political participation. Without political rights, black southerners could not achieve their goals of economic self-sufficiency for themselves and education for their children.

Postwar Reconstruction

Radical Republicans, dominating Congress after the war, aimed to protect and promote the interests of black southerners and to punish white southerners. Reconstruction Acts sent federal troops into the South to maintain order, required former Confederate states to guarantee black male suffrage, and made ratification of the Fourteenth Amendment, which affirmed black people's citizenship, a condition of representation in Congress. Abraham Lincoln had proposed a milder form of Reconstruction, and under his successor Andrew Johnson black rights became the focal point of a contest between the Congress and the executive. In an impeachment trial, the Radical Republicans failed to remove Johnson, but the contest for power between the branches of government—ostensibly about black issues—only diverted federal attention from black people's needs.

In a bitter irony, southern black men, so recently liberated from slavery, had more opportunities for political leadership than did black northerners. As white voters in northern states denied black men the franchise, former abolitionists and black leaders joined in Equal Rights Leagues to fight for full political equality. The 1868 elections brought more moderate Republicans to power, and they proposed the Fifteenth Amendment, prohibiting states from limiting the franchise due to "race, color, or previous condition of servitude." Former Confederate states now had to ratify this new amendment, and Mississippi, one of the first to do so, sent Hiram Revels to the Senate, the first black American in Congress.

The Fourteenth and Fifteenth amendments split the old alliance between black rights and women's rights. The "black men first" strategy specified that males only were citizens, outraging Elizabeth Cady Stanton. Opposing the amendments, Stanton found herself linked to anti-black forces. The issue split the women's rights movement into rival organizations that further split along racial lines, and Mary Ann Shadd Cary and others formed the Colored Woman's Progressive Franchise Association.

Elected Black Leaders

In Congress, Revels's seat was challenged, and he and the six other African Americans found their new power limited. Yet most were pragmatic, using compromise and negotiation to promote education, full citizenship, and patronage for black people. Those who refused to compromise learned that their vote wielded little influence without white allies. On the local level, too, black leaders used compromise and negotiation to gain white support and advance their agenda. Martin Delany, for example, advocated black-white alliances and supported planter Wade Hampton for governor of South Carolina.

In the postwar era, southern politics took one of three forms—the political middle, which, like Hampton, hoped to modernize the South with a diversified economy and new industry; the political right, which sought to hold former slaves in place as laborers on the land; and the radical left, which promoted an alliance of poor people across racial lines and sometimes embraced socialism. Most black leaders, like Delany, cultivated political connections with white moderates; only a few, such as Lucy Parsons, joined the socialist ranks; and all avoided the political right as best they could.

In northern cities, discrimination, especially in transportation, and even violence were evidence that most northern white Americans wanted black people to stay "in their place." But white backlash was much more violent in the South, where the Ku Klux Klan murdered an estimated 20,000 African Americans between 1868 and 1876. Enforcement Acts, aiming to protect black voters against Klan violence, were ineffective, though they did bring black spokesmen like Fortune to Congress to testify.

The Freedmen's Bank

The Freedmen's Bank, chartered by Congress, was intended to help black people save money and secure loans, but when unwise speculation by several white board members caused it to fail and Congress would not save it, the savings of thousands of African Americans evaporated. For many, the failure was evidence that the federal government would not protect black rights.

Washington, DC, in the New National Era

Symbolizing hope and disappointment, the national capital became a magnet for African Americans seeking employment and federal protection. After the war, black people constituted 30 percent of Washington's population. A black elite—about 2 percent of this 30 percent—included professionals, often of mixed race background, from families that had been free for a generation or more. Frederick Douglass, Frances Ellen Watkins Harper, Maria Stewart, and Charlotte Forten were among city's essayists, writers, and public speakers. Shopkeepers and service workers formed the core of the middle class, but more than three-quarters of the city's African Americans were poor, living in alleys in conditions as bleak as endured under slavery. Sojourner Truth and Mary Ann Shadd Cary, Howard University's first female law student, spoke for their interests, arguing for access to education, manual training, and employment. But increasingly, black political leaders—economically well off and circulating in their own social clubs and organizations—lost touch with the needs of ordinary black people.

The District of Columbia's local government offered opportunities for employment, and loyal black Republican supporters were rewarded with political patronage positions. Steady wages allowed for middle-class lifestyles for some and elevated others to elite status. African Americans relocating here and to other cities, too, found they could make some economic progress and begin participating in local politics. Many cities had enough black residents to support a black press.

The End of Reconstruction

As Republican power began to wane in the early 1870s, African American progress began to wane as well. Democrats took over state and local governments in the South, a development hailed by white southerners as "redemption." By the Compromise of 1877, settling the contested presidential election in 1876, federal troops were withdrawn from the South altogether, and federal intervention in southern state affairs ceased. The Supreme Court also limited black advances. In the *Slaughterhouse Cases* it weakened the Fourteenth Amendment by ruling that states had the power to define state citizenship and delineate local civil rights. Furthermore, in 1883 it overturned the Civil Rights Act of 1875, distinguishing between political rights and social rights, which it claimed no power to enforce.

African Americans on the Move

Increasingly, black people chose to leave the South rather than endure escalating violence, which included rape, murder, and mutilation. Some, called Exodusters, took advantage of the 1862 Homestead Act and headed for Kansas, founding all-black towns such as Nicodemus. Others went farther west, to the frontiers in Colorado and North Dakota and even to the Pacific Coast. But some white southerners, seeking to retain the South's cheap labor force, sought to prevent blacks from migrating. Frederick Douglass urged black families to stay in the South, where their numbers might be large enough to exert political power and influence.

Other black Americans, driven by the same hope and frustration that motivated western migration, looked to Africa. Delany revived his dream of claiming a black nationality there, and with AME minister Henry McNeal Turner, he recruited settlers for Liberia. Though their Liberian Exodus Company collapsed, the idea of "returning" to the African homeland remained in the black imagination and future generations would revive it.

LEARNING OBJECTIVES

Students should be able to
- differentiate between the various Reconstruction plans.
- Discuss the controversies over ratification of the Fifteenth Amendment.
- explain the factors leading to the end of Reconstruction.
- discuss the challenges facing ex-slaves and their strategies for coping with them.

IDENTIFICATIONS

Explain the significance of each:

1. Emanuel Fortune

2. Civil Rights Act of 1866

3. Hiram Revels

4. Presidential Reconstruction 1865 - 1867

5. Andrew Johnson

6. Edwin Stanton

7. Impeachment

8. Radical or Congressional Reconstruction

9. Thaddeus Stevens

10. Charles Sumner

11. Fifteenth Amendment

12. Frances Ellen Watkins Harper

13. Blanche K. Bruce

14. Pinckney Benton Stewart Pinchback

15. Wade Hampton

16. Madison Heming

17. Enforcement Acts and/or Klan Acts of 1870 and 1871

18. The Freedmen's Bank

19. African Americans and Washington, DC

20. Howard University

21. John Mercer Langston

22. Freedmen's Hospital

23. Charlotte Forten

24. The Black Elite

25. Sojourner Truth

26. Mary Ann Shadd Cary

27. The Franchise

28. The Disputed Election of 1876

29. Exodusters

30. Nat Love

31. Martin Delaney, Henry McNeal Turner and the *Azor*

MULTIPLE CHOICE QUESTIONS

1. This African American appeared before a congressional committee assigned to investigate Ku Klux Klan threats and violence against black southerners in 1871. In spite of intimidation, this political leader participated in the 1868 constitutional convention that qualified Florida to reenter the Union, and over the next 10 years he served as city marshal, Republican national convention delegate, county commissioner, clerk of the city market, and state legislator. He was
    A. Martin Delaney.
    B. Emanuel Fortune.
    C. Blanche K. Bruce.
    D. Hiram Revels.

2. Presidential Reconstruction took place between 1865 and 1867. Under this plan for restoring the former Confederate states to the Union, President Lincoln and his successor favored a lenient policy whereby once a southern state ratified the Thirteenth Amendment and a portion of the white voters took an oath of allegiance to the Union, then that state could come back into the Union with no further punishment. All of the following facts about Presidential Reconstruction are true EXCEPT:
    A. By December, 1865, most of the former Confederate states had been restored to the Union.
    B. Many former Confederate officeholders were sitting in Congress to help govern a country that they had just spent the past four years trying to destroy when Congress convened in December, 1865.
    C. Local white political leaders passed laws called "Black Codes" that severely limited the freedom of the newly freed blacks.
    D. The Freedmen's Bureau established schools, provided assistance, and helped African Americans adjust to the new life.
    E. By 1866 African Americans could sue in court, could vote, and could hold public office in most Southern states.

3. What was the first concern of many African Americans once they achieved freedom?
   A. Retaliating against former masters
   B. Reuniting with lost family members
   C. Forming churches
   D. Moving to the Northern cities

4. Who became President after Lincoln was assassinated in April, 1865?
   A. Andrew Johnson
   B. Lyndon Baines Johnson
   C. Andrew Jackson
   D. William Tecumseh Sherman
   E. Ulysses S. Grant

5. On what grounds did the Radical Republicans in Congress bring impeachment proceedings against Lincoln's successor?
   A. The president tried to remove his secretary of war Edwin Stanton. This removal was in violation of the recently passed Tenure of Office Act.
   B. The president promised to restore confiscated land to former Confederate owners - land that had been parceled out to newly freed blacks.
   C. The president vetoed Congress' Civil Rights Act of 1866 – an act that offered limited legal rights to African Americans.
   D. He also vetoed a congressional vote to renew the charter for the Freedmen's Bureau.
   E. All of the above.

6. He was the first president to be impeached by the House of Representatives. He was one vote shy of being removed from office by the Senate. Who was he?
   A. Andrew Jackson
   B. Ulysses S. Grant
   C. Andrew Johnson
   D. William Jefferson Clinton
   E. William Tecumseh Sherman

7. In 1867 Congress passed three new Reconstruction Acts that brought on what is known as Radical or Congressional Reconstruction. Which of the following provisions were part of Congressional Reconstruction?
   A. The South was divided into five military districts, sending federal troops to maintain order and protect freed people.
   B. Former Confederate states were required to hold conventions to draft constitutions that guaranteed black male suffrage.
   C. Former Confederate states could send representatives to Congress only after state legislatures had ratified the Fourteenth Amendment.
   D. All of the above
   E. Only A and B are correct.

8. Charles Sumner and Thaddeus Stevens were the two leading Radical Republicans in Congress. Stevens in the House and Sumner in the Senate paved the way for the passage of the Fourteenth and Fifteenth Amendments to the Constitution. Which of the following leaders of the period are **NOT** correctly paired with their achievements?
    A. Hiram Revels and Blanche K. Bruce – African American U.S. Senators from the state of Mississippi
    B. Martin Delaney and Henry McNeal Turner – 'Back to Africa' movement
    C. Frances Ellen Watkins Harper and Mary Ann Shadd Cary – Black female Civil rights advocates
    D. Charlotte Forten and Sojourner Truth – African American pioneers who became Exodusters

9. The Fifteenth Amendment to the Constitution provided for which of the following?
    A. Abolition of slavery
    B. Male Negro suffrage
    C. Negro citizenship
    D. An end to segregation

10. During Congressional or radical Reconstruction, African Americans participated for the first time in local, state and national politics. In Congress eventually 22 African Americans served – two in the Senate and 20 in the House. What is the highest state office to which a black man was elected in the South during Reconstruction?
    A. Governor
    B. State senator
    C. Lieutenant Governor
    D. Blacks were not elected to any state offices.

11. Which of the following statements is **NOT** true about black officeholders during Reconstruction?
    A. They were always well-qualified for their office.
    B. Only a small minority had attended college.
    C. Some had been free before the war; some had been slaves.
    D. Farmers and workers were well represented.

12. Which of the following men was the offspring of a union between a slave woman, Sally, and her white master, Thomas Jefferson, who went on to become the third President of the United States?
    A. John Mercer Langston
    B. Madison Heming
    C. Wade Hampton
    D. P.B.S. Pinchback

13. The Ku Klux Klan, which quickly evolved into a terrorist hate group, was founded in 1866, in Pulaski, Tennessee. According to some sources, shortly after the war's end, idle planters and their sons were initiating some of their peers into a secret organization when they discovered by accident that the hoods and robes worn during pledge night frightened and/or intimidated a group of blacks. The organization grew and continued to harass anyone who supported Reconstruction, blacks being their main targets. Which of the following statements concerning the actions of the KKK is <u>NOT</u> true?
    A. Klan activity and membership was generally popular only among the poor whites who resented both elite whites and blacks.
    B. Klan actions frequently helped to eliminate Republican leadership.
    C. Klan members conducted campaigns of violence, murder and terrorism against blacks.
    D. All of the above are true.

14. What was the main problem in enforcing laws against the Klan?
    A. Since no terrorist groups had existed before, there were no laws to deal with them.
    B. Many times, local law enforcement or white troops sided with the Klan against the blacks.
    C. There were only a very small number of men in the Klan, and they always remained secret and hidden from prosecution.
    D. The Klan's actions were almost invisible since no one reported news of the terrorism.

15. Which of the following statements about the Enforcement Acts of 1870 and 1871 are true?
    A. They made it a federal crime to interfere with someone's right to vote.
    B. They authorized the president to send in federal troops if necessary.
    C. They authorized the president to suspend the writ of habeas corpus if necessary.
    D. All of the above are true.

16. Why did the Freedmen's Savings Bank fail?
    A. The bank's black board of directors had little direct knowledge of banking practices.
    B. The bank had no support from the black community.
    C. The stock market at that point was very weak and fluctuated wildly.
    D. Some white board members invested unsoundly, and lost everything in the Panic of 1873.

17. The seat of both hope and disappointment, Washington, DC, became a magnet for black Americans. By 1870, African Americans constituted more than 30 percent of the capital city's population of 132,000. Which of the following statements about African Americans in DC are true?

    A. Drawn by the federal government and Howard University, many accomplished African Americans settled in the capital city. Frederick Douglass moved to DC and started a newspaper, then later moved into government service. John Mercer Langston moved there to direct the law curriculum at Howard University and also later got involved in government service. There were many other affluent blacks who did likewise.

    B. Many intellectuals, such as black poets, essayists, novelists, and public speakers were drawn to DC by intellectuals who were already there. The black elite of Washington, DC – around two percent of the city's black population- consisted of lawyers, doctors, teachers, publishers and business owners.

    C. Shopkeepers and service workers formed the core of DC's black middle class. They enjoyed the chance to rub shoulders not only with DC's black politicians and intellectuals but also with renowned social activists.

    D. More than three quarters of DC's black families lived in alleys next to large houses where they served as laundresses, porters, handymen, and domestic servants. In the crowded alleys near the Capitol and along the Potomac River lived those who worked in government service.

    E. All of the above.

18. Radical Reconstruction had brought important gains to black southerners: schools, economic possibilities, and the franchise. In 1875, Congress passed a Civil Rights act that banned discrimination in public places throughout the country. By 1876, many white Northerners had grown tired of the plight of the newly freed blacks; and the Presidential election of the year showed just that. Because neither candidate received the required number of electoral votes, the election was thrown in to the House of Representatives. As a result of the Compromise of 1877, Rutherford B. Hayes, a Republican, won. Which of the following concessions did Hayes have to make in order to win?

    A. He would agree to end Reconstruction by pulling military troops out of the southern states.

    B. White southerners would be able to control local elections and would be able to make local ordinances controlling such issues as black employment contracts and racial separation.

    C. Federal intervention in southern state affairs would cease and Hayes would appoint at least one southerner to the president's cabinet.

    D. A and B are correct but C is not.

    E. A, B, and C are correct.

19.   Who were the Exodusters?
      A. 40,000 African Americans who left the south and migrated to Kansas between
          the years 1870 and 1880
      B. Black people, likening themselves to the biblical Hebrews that fled from
          bondage in Egypt, who went west with groups financed by the Kansas Exodus
          Joint Stock Company
      C. African Americans who took advantage of the Homestead Act and moved,
          despite opposition from southern whites, to Nicodemus, Kansas, establishing
          the all-black town there
      D. All of the above
      E. B and C are correct

20.   All of the following African Americans moved to the western frontier, found adventure
      and/or fortune in places such as Nebraska, Colorado, North Dakota or along the Pacific
      coast. Who among the following did NOT settle in the West?
      A. Isom Dart
      B. Nat Love
      C. Nancy Lewis
      D. Biddy Mason
      E. All of the above-mentioned colorful characters lived on the Western
          Frontier.

THOUGHT QUESTIONS

1.   Evaluate the successes and/or failures of Reconstruction based on the economic, political,
     and social changes in the lives of black people.

2.   How did African Americans attempt to work within the political system during
     Reconstruction to effect change? How were they limited?

3.   How was the Freedmen's Bureau both a positive and a negative influence for the newly
     freed blacks? Why did Bureau members seem to want blacks to stay in
     agricultural positions?

ANSWER KEY MULTIPLE CHOICE QUESTIONS

1. B
2. E
3. B
4. A
5. E
6. C
7. D
8. D
9. B
10. C
11. A
12. B
13. A
14. B
15. D
16. D
17. E
18. E
19. D
20. E

CHAPTER 12 *The Post-Reconstruction Era*

CHAPTER SUMMARY

Opening Vignette: Booker T. Washington Teaches Black Self-Sufficiency

Like millions of southern black people, Booker T. Washington began life in poverty. At Hampton Institute, where he worked as a janitor to help pay his way, he learned a recipe for success: manual labor, hygiene, thrift, and deference to white people. Later, as head of Tuskegee Institute, he taught this formula. With his own life story as an example, he used images of climbing and lifting to describe black progress and social responsibility.

Rebuilding the South

In the post-Reconstruction South, white and black farmers found themselves locked in a vicious cycle of poverty, even black landowners like Isaiah Montgomery who had tenant farmers. Following the end of the plantation economy, three new forms of agriculture emerged: *sharecopping*, in which the landlord provided seed, housing, and tools in return for a share of the crop; *share tenancy*, in which landlords provided the housing but tenants chose the crop, secured the seed, and set their own schedule for harvesting and selling; and *tenant farming*, in which tenants paid cash to rent farmland. Most farmers, even landlords, carried debt, called *crop lien*, borrowed against the next harvest. Inherited debt shackled most black families to the land as tightly as slavery had done. The situation was exacerbated by the reliance on barter rather than cash, which made it easy for those who had wealth, land, or literacy to swindle those who did not. In most southern states, only 25 percent of black residents owned land. As plots in the South multiplied and decreased in size, southern farmers lagged behind, lacking land and capital for the advances in mechanized farming that boosted agriculture on the Great Plains. Although some capitalists sought to modernize the South and a few cities boasted factories—steel in Birmingham, railroads in Memphis, tobacco in Richmond, and textile mills in Montgomery and Greensboro—the bartering and economic interdependence that had defined the southern economy under slavery persisted in the post-Reconstruction era.

By the early 1880s, the federal government withdrew from aiding southern freedmen. Supreme Court rulings excluded black Americans from juries and upheld segregation laws, called Jim Crow. By 1890 most northern states also had laws and customs segregating black from white. Charles Darwin's theory of evolution seemed to justify social inequality: in a competitive marketplace, only the most vigorous survived, and deserved to. Its adjunct, social Darwinism, justified nonintervention on behalf of the poor, and eugenics posited notions of innate racial traits and racial hierarchies. White people claimed a "noble burden" to colonize Africa and Christianize backward regions. The exclusion of Chinese immigrants and the exploitation of black labor were also justified.

As federal protection waned, so did national black leadership. One new leader was Washington, who shaped his understanding of southern poverty into a broad social philosophy that accepted segregation in return for work and protection from violence. Tuskegee flourished, drawing white support by producing graduates with agricultural, craft, and industrial skills, a strong work ethic, and a commitment to lift others out of poverty.

Education: Making a Living and a Life

The American Missionary Association, Freedmen's Bureau, and church denominations had started black schools throughout the South. Many were maintained by northern philanthropists and southern white donors eager to secure skilled workers. Fisk College's Jubilee singers introduced the world to slave songs, raising enough money to get the school out of debt. Fisk had an academic curriculum, as did Virginia State College, where John Mercer Langston was the first president. W.E.B. Du Bois argued that only a liberal arts curriculum could shape African American boys into men, and women who studied to be teachers wanted to impart more than manual skills. Whether the curriculum was vocational or academic, these schools fostered personal and black pride. By century's end, the issue of whether black children should be educated in integrated or all-black schools was moot, as separate schools became the norm everywhere.

The Lure of Cities

African Americans, though less than 10 percent of northern urbanites in the 1880s, found that cities offered them economic and social opportunities. Black communities thrived in cities along waterways and railroad lines, where new black towns were established, such as Mississippi's Mound Bayou, led by Montgomery. When enough black people settled near each other, viable black businesses developed; Maggie Lena Walker's bank in Richmond is an example. Urban life also enabled black churches to flourish as places of worship, social centers, forums for politics, and offices for community services such as burial insurance and savings and loan institutions. Some cities developed highly stratified societies. Black communities in Philadelphia and Topeka had distinct layers, divided by class. Federal appointments attracted many black men and women to Washington, D.C.

The Economics and Politics of Unity

As the South industrialized, unions, especially the Knights of Labor, sought to unite black and white workers in its goal of replacing capitalism with a system in which workers owned the means of production. Labor leader Frank Ferrell helped increase the Knights' black membership, while Lucy Parsons, whose husband was executed following the Haymarket Riots, fought for workers' rights for half a century, speaking at the founding of the Industrial Workers of the World. In the wake of Haymarket, the Knights weakened.

Urban labor union activism was mirrored by farmers who established alliances or cooperatives to share the costs of equipment and resist the high costs of shipping. The Colored Farmers National Alliance and Cooperative Union, representing thousands of black farmers in a dozen states, joined with white farmers Alliances in fights against railroad monopolies. These alliances fed into the new Populist Party, which also embraced women's suffrage advocates and urban reformers with radical ideas about redistributing wealth and restricting the power of corporations and railroads. Following the Panic of 1893 and the failure of Democrat William Jennings Bryan, whom they endorsed, to win the presidency in 1896, the Populists faded away.

Finding a Place to Uplift the Race

Subjected to racial discrimination, poverty, and isolation from mainstream America, black southerners often moved, some within the South but others out west. Some 20,000 black soldiers served at western military posts; other men were miners. Some African Americans joined in the land rush following the opening of Oklahoma Territory to homesteading, including the Franklin family, ancestors of renowned historian John Hope Franklin. In Iowa, George Washington Carver studied chemistry and botany at a white agricultural college, then joined Tuskegee's faculty, where he trained black scientists and helped revitalize southern agriculture by conducting research on peanuts, boll weevil infestation, and tobacco diseases, and instituting crop rotation.

A few black Americans looked again toward Africa. Black scholar George Washington Williams wrote on Christianity in Africa and helped Belgium's King Leopold Christianize the Congo until he realized that this scheme was a fraud that exploited and sometimes enslaved African workers. Edward Blyden and Henry McNeal Turner also promoted the Christianization and colonization of Africa. Over many years, a few black Americans went to Liberia.

Terror and Accommodation

Increasingly, white southerners used the lynching of black men as a means of enforcing racial inequality. Those who ran successful businesses, stood up to white insults, ran for office, or risked voting were singled out. One was Thomas Moss, a storeowner in Memphis. His death inspired Ida B. Wells to begin a campaign against lynching, first in the Memphis paper she co-owned and then in T. Thomas Fortune's *New York Age.*

In 1895, at the Cotton States and International Exposition in Atlanta, Washington gave a notable address that became known as the Atlanta Compromise. Believing that the destinies of black and white southerners were intertwined, he urged southern factory owners to hire black Americans, whom they would find "faithful, law-abiding and unresentful." He also urged black Americans to "cast down your bucket where you are" and accept racial segregation. Fortune praised Washington's speech, as did Montgomery. But many African Americans distanced themselves from Washington and his ideas.

LEARNING OBJECTIVES

Students should be able to
- describe the economic situations of free blacks in the South.
- identify the ideas of Darwin, social Darwinism, and eugenics, and assess their impact on views of black Americans.
- discuss the importance of education for freedmen and women.
- explain the ways in which black Americans resisted white terror.

IDENTIFICATION TERMS

Explain the significance of each of the following:

1. Sharecropping

2. Tenant farming

3. Crop lien

4. Jim Crow

5. Booker T. Washington

6. Tuskegee Institute

7. Social Darwinism

8. Ida B. Wells

9. American Missionary Association (AMA)

10. Fisk Jubilee Singers

11. W.E.B. Du Bois

12. Charlotte Ray

13. Maggie Lena Walker

14. Robert Reed Church

15. Knights of Labor

16. Lucy Parsons

17. Populism

18. George Washington Carver

19. George Washington Williams

20. Henry McNeal Turner

21. Lynching

22. Atlanta Compromise

23. Eugenics

24. Ninth and Tenth Cavalry

25. Henry Johnson

26. John Alexander

27. Mound Bayou

MULTIPLE CHOICE QUESTIONS

1. African American farmers participated in all of the following types of agriculture <u>EXCEPT</u>
    A. sharecropping.
    B. share tenancy.
    C. tenant farming.
    D. serfdom.

2. African American agriculture was characterized by all of the following <u>EXCEPT</u>
    A. debt cycle.
    B. foreign competition.
    C. lack of cash.
    D. large landholdings.

3. The term *Jim Crow* refers to
    A. segregation laws of the South.
    B. a type of popular dance.
    C. the racial relations of the Old South.
    D. African American soldiers.

4. In which year did the Supreme Court limit equal accommodation laws?
    A. 1877
    B. 1880
    C. 1883
    D. 1896

5. Booker T. Washington preferred what type of education for African Americans?
    A. Liberal Arts
    B. Practical Training
    C. Apprenticeships
    D. Fine Arts

6. Booker T. Washington believed that race progress would come after African Americans did all of the following EXCEPT
    A. refined their speech.
    B. learned a skill.
    C. cleaned themselves up.
    D. integrated into society.

7. The anti-lynching crusade in American was essentially led by
    A. Booker T. Washington.
    B. W.E.B. Du Bois.
    C. Ida B. Wells.
    D. Henry M. Turner.

8. There were several liberal arts schools formed by churches and the AMA during the post-war period. Which of the following is NOT one of them?
    A. Fisk College
    B. Tuskegee Institute
    C. Howard College
    D. Spelman College

9. African American women took advantage of educational opportunities. Who was the first Black female lawyer?
    A. Charlotte Ray
    B. Mary Ann Shadd Cary
    C. Lucy Moten
    D. Ida B. Wells

10. During the 1880s African Americans left the rural areas of the south and moved to urban areas to take advantage of job opportunities. All of the following became successful entrepreneurs EXCEPT
    A. Maggie Lena Walker.
    B. Robert R. Church.
    C. Henry Clay Williams.
    D. James Garfield.

11. All of the following states had successful Black towns EXCEPT
    A. New Jersey.
    B. Mississippi.
    C. Florida.
    D. Massachusetts.

12. What were the major factors that blocked African Americans from being effective in the labor and Populist movement?
    A. White hostility
    B. Lack of opportunities
    C. Opposition to union leadership
    D. Nothing in common with Whites

13. Which of the following BEST describes the African American experience as it relates to westward expansion?
    A. They found it nearly impossible to find opportunities.
    B. There were very few African Americans who went West.
    C. African Americans found greater freedom and more opportunities but still faced opposition.
    D. They were able to forge alliances with Native Americans.

14. All of the following were major aspects of the Atlanta Compromise EXCEPT
    A. African Americans would remain in the South.
    B. acceptance of segregation.
    C. Whites were to treat Blacks fairly.
    D. Blacks would elect several leaders.

15. Social Darwinists and Eugenicists believed that
    A. African Americans and Whites were essentially equal people.
    B. Blacks were lazy and could not compete with Whites.
    C. Africa was once a great society but that they had forfeited their greatness.
    D. African Americans were genetically inferior and had to be helped by Whites.

THOUGHT QUESTIONS

1. Why were labor organizations fearful of fostering racial cooperation in the south?

2. How would you explain the development of segregation and the increase of anti-black violence in light of recent laws proclaiming legal equality?

3. Considering the time period and White attitudes towards African Americans, was Booker T. Washington's program the best hope for African American progress?

4. Was African American dedication to agriculture good for African American economic development?

5. How would you evaluate African American Westward expansion?

6. What were the major imperatives for creating all-Black towns?

7. What do we learn about attitudes towards women from Alexander Crummell's plea to Black women?

8. Would you describe Anna Julia Cooper's words as hopeful or frustrated?

ANSWER KEY MULTIPLE CHOICE QUESTIONS

1. D
2. D
3. A
4. C
5. B
6. D
7. C
8. B
9. A
10. D
11. D
12. A
13. C
14. D
15. D

CHAPTER 13 *"Colored" Becomes "Negro" in the Progressive Era*

CHAPTER SUMMARY

Opening Vignette: Mary Church Terrell and the NACW

In 1896, representatives of 40 black women's clubs met to form the National Association of Colored Women (NACW). They honored Harriet Tubman for her leadership in the slave past and selected Mary Church Terrell as president. Adopting "lifting as we climb" as their motto, they echoed Booker T. Washington and the progressive spirit by pledging to build a strong national community through a focus on children and home life.

Racial Segregation

That same year, the Supreme Court upheld the Louisiana Separate Car Act, thus shaping American racial policies and limiting black people's civil rights for more than half a century. Homer Plessy, a New Orleans Creole with one black great-grandfather, had challenged the law by sitting in a car reserved for white people. He and his supporters, the New Orleans Citizens Committee, welcomed the arrest that followed, hoping to use public opinion and the courts to secure equal access to public services. But the district court declared that Louisiana's law *did* treat black and white people equally: it prohibited both from sitting in integrated cars. The Supreme Court agreed, stating in *Plessy v. Ferguson* that as long as equal services were provided for black and white people, states could require racial segregation. As a consequence, many states and localities, in the South but also in the North, passed segregation laws that kept white and black people apart in schools, libraries, prisons, hospitals, cemeteries, hotels, theaters, restaurants, and jobs and neighborhoods. Rejecting the notion that enforced separation marked "the colored race with a badge of inferiority," the Court made "separate but equal" the law of the land. Two years later it upheld Mississippi's poll tax, opening the way for taxes and tests, such as "grandfather clauses," that would disfranchise African Americans.

In these rulings the court enacted into public policy ideas about racial hierarchies stemming from Social Darwinism and the pseudoscience of eugenics. Progressive aims to improve civilization through social management merged with these ideas to uphold white supremacy. Discouraged, many African Americans concluded that Washington was right—that they had best concentrate on economic progress, not legal and political equality. They accepted the designation *negro*, the term scientists used to identify black people; however, they insisted on capitalizing the "N" as a mark of dignity.

The Problem of the Color Line

"The problem of the twentieth century is the problem of the color line" announced W.E.B. Du Bois at the 1900 Pan-African Conference in London. For him, the line that divided black from white in the United States was one manifestation of a problem that was global. As European nations sanctioned imperialism and the division of Africa into white-ruled colonies, he understood that racism in international politics meant ruthless economic exploitation of dark-skinned peoples. In Pan-Africanism, he sought to unite blacks worldwide in an international stand against racism.

The recent Spanish-American War exemplified white arrogance that dark-skinned peoples were incapable of self-government and required white direction. America's stated purpose of liberating Cuba and the Philippines from Spain was belied when U.S. troops continued to occupy the Philippines despite an uprising that took 14,000 Filipino lives. At home, the war had divided black Americans between those who urged loyalty and those who argued that they were as much in need of independence as the Cubans. The nature of the color line was made clear when an entire black regiment, with many soldiers recently returned from the Philippines, was dishonorably discharged following a controversial shooting incident in Brownsville, Texas. Though President Theodore Roosevelt had raised black hopes by inviting Washington to dine in the White House, he dashed them by prohibiting trial or appeal in this case.

Accommodation or Agitation?

The Brownsville incident signified African Americans' political powerlessness and internal divisions. Washington refrained from public comment, and his outward passivity weakened his singular influence. While Washington continued to help black southerners acquire vocational skills, to court white philanthropists, and to promote black enterprise through Republican Party connections, Du Bois now challenged his strategy of accommodation, claiming it kept African Americans from seeking political power and protesting racial injustice. In *The Souls of Black Folk,* Du Bois contended that the American Negro "ever feels his Twoness—an American, a Negro." He ascribed a lyrical, mystical quality to black consciousness and called on the "the Talented Tenth" to lead the race. The rivalry between Washington and Du Bois would dominate black discourse until Washington's death in 1915.

In July 1905, Du Bois and other black intellectuals such as journalist William Monroe Trotter and Morehouse College president John Hope met in Niagara Falls, Ontario, to formalize their commitment to agitation as a means for securing equal rights for black citizens. Catalyzed by a race riot in Springfield, Illinois, in 1908, the Niagara Movement attracted the support of white Progressives in the founding of the National Association for the Advancement of Colored People in 1910. The organization aimed to initiate test cases that would force the courts to end racial segregation. Du Bois became editor of its magazine, *Crisis.*

Black Culture

Appreciation of black culture crossed the color line. International audiences had thrilled to performances of the Fisk Jubilee Singers, and now Scott Joplin's popular ragtime compositions made him the first black American to earn a living writing music. Paul Laurence Dunbar's poetry reached appreciative audiences, inspiring others, such as James Weldon Johnson. In sports, too, individual black athletes excelled. Cyclist Major Taylor competed with white cyclists and founded the Colored Wheelman's Association. Baseball, segregated by 1900, offered opportunities for standout players. Boxer Jack Johnson became a hero to black Americans when he won the heavyweight championship title. White fans searched for a "Great White Hope" to reclaim the title for the white race.

Black Progress

After Philip A. Payton's Afro-American Realty Company helped black Americans secure rentals in Harlem, this section of New York became a center of black cultural improvement. Here the NAACP set up its office, and the National Urban League, representing a broader spectrum of black society, was founded to tackle issues of working-class city life. The White Rose Mission offered settlement house services to newcomers. But Progressive institutions that sought to improve the social and economic environment were not limited to Harlem. In cities everywhere, churches performed social as well as religious missions, serving as recreation centers, political forums, employment agencies, savings and loan institutions, and incubators of black talent. College fraternities and sororities facilitated business partnerships and social networks. All these organizations instilled black pride.

Leaders with new focuses emerged in Harlem. A. Philip Randolph studied politics and labor organizing. "Chief" Alfred Charles Sam promoted trade between Africans and African Americans and the Christianization of Africa. Du Bois, Carter G. Woodson, and Alain Locke founded the Negro Historical Society of Research, and Woodson established the Association for the Study of Negro Life and History, which celebrated the achievements of black Americans in the new *Journal of Negro History.* Arthur Schomburg collected literary works and visual art by people of African descent. And in 1914 Marcus Garvey established the Universal Negro Improvement Association.

The "New Abolition"

As violence against black people continued, black leaders advocated four options: emigration, separate communities within the United States, agitation for full civil and political rights, or accommodation to white supremacy. Du Bois chose agitation, and after 1912 he and the NAACP were assisted by Joel Spingarn, who inaugurated the "New Abolition" movement to abolish segregation. Simultaneously, the NAACP worked to remove legal obstacles, and in three successful cases it challenged housing discrimination and outlawed Oklahoma's grandfather clause. After Washington died, Du Bois sought to end divisions among black leaders at the Amenia Conference. In its statement affirming both liberal and industrial education and a unified attack on segregation and lynching, Trotter perceived a "spring-time of the race's hopes in America."

LEARNING OBJECTIVES

Students should be able to
- describe the goals and tactics of black political organizations that formed during this era.
- examine the arguments of the Supreme Court in the *Plessy v. Ferguson* decision.
- compare the different political strategies of Washington and W.E.B. Du Bois.
- discuss the strides made by black musicians, writers, and athletes.

IDENTIFICATIONS

Explain the significance of each of the following:

1. Mary Church Terrell

2. National Association of Colored Women (NACW)

3. Homer Plessy

4. Poll Tax

5. Literacy Test

6. Grandfather Clause

7. *Plessy v Ferguson* ruling

8. Progressives

9. use of the term "Negro"

10. W.E.B. Du Bois

11. Pan Africanism

12. American Negro Academy

13. Brownsville Incident

14. Niagara Movement

15. William Monroe Trotter

16. NAACP

17. John Hope

18. Buck Franklin

19. Scott Joplin

20. Paul Lawrence Dunbar

21. Major Taylor

22. Jack Johnson

23. Charles S. Smith

24. Harlem

25. Urban League

26. Alice Ruth Moore

27. National Baptist Publishing Board

28. National Negro Doll Company

29. National Afro-American Press Association

30. T. Thomas Fortune

31. A. Philip Randolph

32. "Chief" Alfred Charles Sam

33. Carter G. Woodson

34. ASNLH

35. Arthur Schomburg

36. Marcus Garvey

37. Joel Spingarn

38. Ragtime

MULTIPLE CHOICE QUESTIONS

1. When Homer Plessy challenged the segregation laws of Louisiana in 1892, he was supported by which organization?
    A. The National Association for the Advancement of Colored People
    B. The National Urban League
    C. New Orleans Citizens' Committee
    D. National Association of Colored Women

2. The laws which mandated the separation of the races were referred to as
    A. Jim Crow laws.
    B. separation ordinances.
    C. Whites' Only Rules.
    D. Black Codes.

3. The organization founded by Carter G. Woodson to study the African American past was called
   A. Schomburg Center for Afro American Research.
   B. Association for the Study of Negro Life and History.
   C. The Woodson Center for Negro Study.
   D. the Harvard University WEB Du Bois Institute of Afro-American Research.

4. All of the following opposed Booker T. Washington's program EXCEPT
   A. W.E.B. Du Bois.
   B. William Monroe Trotter.
   C. Ida B. Wells.
   D. Emmett J. Scott.

5. All of the following are Black fraternities and sororities founded at Howard University EXCEPT
   A. Omega Psi Phi.
   B. Phi Beta Sigma.
   C. Alpha Kappa Alpha.
   D. Alpha Phi Alpha.

6. Boxer Jack Johnson dominated the boxing world for several years. However, most white Americans hated him because he
   A. defeated former champ Jim Jefferies.
   B. dated and married White women.
   C. claimed to be White.
   D. never fought a quality opponent.

7. Richard Henry Boyd established the National Baptist Publishing Board to
   A. publish African American religious material.
   B. print a Black Baptist magazine.
   C. take the burden off of White Baptist publishers.
   D. compete with the AME Church.

8. Scott Joplin distinguished himself as the creative genius of which musical genre?
   A. Jazz
   B. Rock and Roll
   C. Ragtime
   D. Gospel

9. The first African American to make a living from his writing was
   A. Frederick Douglass.
   B. Dr. WEB. Du Bois.
   C. J. Rosamond Johnson.
   D. Paul Lawrence Dunbar.

10. Philip A. Payton is most associated with developing affordable housing for African Americans in which city?

    A. New York

    B. Philadelphia

    C. Boston

    D. Chicago

11. African American distinguished themselves in several sports during the late nineteenth century and early twentieth century. Which of the following was <u>NOT</u> an example of an African American sports hero?

    A. Spottswood Poles

    B. Charles S. Smith

    C. Major Taylor

    D. Jack Johnson

12. The National Urban League differed from the NAACP in that it

    A. was an integrated organization.

    B. was a national organization.

    C. concentrated on helping working-class people adapt to city life.

    D. hoped to improve Black life.

13. African Americans developed their own voice through newspapers during this period. Which of the following was <u>NOT</u> an African American newspaper?

    A *New York Age*

    B. *Chicago Defender*

    C. *New York Post*

    D. *Pittsburgh Courier*

14. The Niagara Movement and NAACP both wanted all the following for African Americans <u>EXCEPT</u>

    A. an end to segregation and discrimination.

    B full citizenship rights.

    C. more support for Booker T. Washington.

    D. protected voting rights.

15. The Akim Trading Company was created to establish commercial relations between African Americans and Africa. Who founded this company?

    A. A. Philip Randolph

    B. "Chief" Alfred Charles Sam

    C. Marcus Garvey

    D. Alonzo Ransier

THOUGHT QUESTIONS

1. What was the impact of the Progressive movement on African Americans?

2. Discuss the African American reaction to the development of segregation in the U.S.
3. What were the major organizations African Americans founded to fight discrimination, segregation, and racism during the early twentieth century?

4. Describe the way African Americans attempted to link their struggle for equal rights with their African heritage.

5. Discuss the intellectual debate within the African American community over the names *Negro* and *Colored.*

6. Discuss the mixed emotions African American soldiers had in fighting the Spanish-American War and later the Philippine rebellion.

7. Describe the opposition to Booker T. Washington's program of accommodation.

8. How did African Americans distinguish themselves socially, culturally, artistically, and athletically during the late nineteenth and early twentieth centuries?

9. How did urbanization change the life and struggles of African Americans?

10. How did African Americans attempt to present a united front after 1915?

ANSWER KEY MULTIPLE CHOICE QUESTIONS

1. C
2. A
3. B
4. D
5. D
6. B
7. A
8. C
9. D
10. A
11. B
12. C
13. C
14. C
15. B

CHAPTER 14 *The Making of a "New Negro": World War I to the Great Depression*

CHAPTER SUMMARY

Opening Vignette: To the European Front

The diary of First Lieutenant Thomas Jones, a physician in the all-black 368th Infantry serving in France in World War I, reveals the warm welcome African American troops received from the French, the horror of trench warfare, and the vicious racism of white American comrades in arms.

"Over There" . . . and Back Here

The black unity W.E.B. Du Bois had worked for evaporated when the United States entered World War I in April 1917. Many questioned whether black men should go to war and join a segregated military to make the rest of the world "safe for democracy" when they did not have full political and social rights at home. At first Du Bois believed national unity should come first, anticipating that military service abroad would earn African Americans respect and legal equality at home. William Monroe Trotter, on the other hand, urged black Americans to boycott the military until it agreed to integrated units and black officers.

Simultaneously, racial tensions mounted. In the summer of 1917, dozens of Twenty-fourth Infantry soldiers were court-martialed for disobeying Houston's Jim Crow laws. Overseas, black units were criticized for poor training and ridiculed by their white officers; close quarters promoted racial abuse. Though some units served with distinction, reports in the United States seldom acknowledged black soldiers' bravery. Returning troops were not welcomed. Du Bois was now convinced that they should "return fighting." In "If We Must Die," poet Claude McKay urged them to "fight back."

Demographic changes also heightened racial tensions. After war began in Europe, but before the United States entered, war industries in need of workers drew waves of African Americans out of the South. Historians call this the Great Migration, and by 1930 half of black Americans had left the rural South; a large number of these, about 2 million, migrated to northern cities. They were escaping terror and poverty, made worse by boll weevil infestations, and seeking economic opportunity, but white workers' fear of competition translated into continuing discrimination and intimidation. In 1916 in East St. Louis, a riot took eight white lives. In 1921, a riot in Tulsa, provoked by a false rape accusation, took 50 black lives.

Lynching increased too. Though the NAACP lobbied for the Dyer anti-lynching bill, Congress, paralyzed by a Senate filibuster, took no action. Meanwhile the Ku Klux Klan revived, now targeting not only black people but Jews, Catholics, and dark-skinned immigrants from Europe. Interracial violence peaked in the summer of 1919, but most Americans were more aware of the Red Scare, in which the attorney-general targeted socialists, anarchists, and labor radicals thought to have connections with Russia's new communist regime. African Americans were suspect, and the Justice Department investigated *Crisis* and other black periodicals. Socialism appealed to some African Americans, including A. Philip Randolph, founder of the Brotherhood of Sleeping Car Porters, especially for its tenet that socioeconomic inequality was a greater problem than racial differences.

The Challenge of Garveyism

Marcus Garvey drew inspiration from Booker T. Washington, and his Universal Negro Improvement Association drew its fast-growing following from the working-class black people newly arrived in northern cities. In contrast to Du Bois and other intellectuals affiliated with the NAACP, who promoted equal access for African Americans within the existing system, Garvey promoted separatism, with the UNIA as an umbrella for black economic, philosophical, social, and religious enterprises. The message was not only self-help but self-reliance. Setting a goal of "Negro producers, Negro distributors, Negro consumers," Garvey conceived his "Negro nation" as a global political and economic network. The UNIA had a commercial shipping operation, factories producing uniforms for its recruiters and nurses, a laundry, black doll factories, Caribbean grocery stores, restaurants, a hotel, and a print shop. It owned property in Harlem, Philadelphia, Chicago, and Pittsburgh. By 1925, it claimed 6 million members worldwide with branches in Central and South America, Britain, and West and South Africa.

Like the eugenicists, Garvey advocated racial purity, but his collaborations with like-minded Klan leaders outraged supporters and opponents alike. The NAACP and Urban League were critical of Garvey's programs (especially as their memberships declined and their programs lost momentum), and federal officials, alarmed by his defiant posture, watched him closely. In 1922 he was convicted of mail fraud. Though his influence dwindled, the UNIA, as a large and powerful movement of black Americans foreshadowed the later civil rights movement.

New Beginnings in the City

In 1920, only one-third of the nation's black population lived in cities; but by 1930, almost half were urban dwellers. City life opened new doors. With jobs in industry and domestic service, black workers were no long trapped in the perpetual debt and barter typical of rural areas. Their migration also meant a transition to cash wages that allowed them to set their own priorities in spending. Black women outnumbered white women in the workforce, and increasing numbers found careers in nursing, social work, and teaching. Homeownership reached an average of 25 to 30 percent. Everywhere, the rising standard of living inspired feelings of optimism and black unity.

With the growth of all-black neighborhoods and the movement of white people to the suburbs, many African Americans had minimal contact with white people. As segregation became more entrenched, it became increasingly difficult for most black and white Americans to imagine the humanity of the other race. Racial tensions and patterns were the subject of scientific investigations that expanded on Du Bois's pioneering study of Philadelphia and built a tradition of black sociological studies.

The Harlem Renaissance and the "New Negro"

In 1925, scholar Alain Locke announced the arrival of a "New Negro," energized by "a new vision of opportunity, of social and economic freedom." His *The New Negro,* aimed to free black Americans from stereotypes. Benjamin Brawley's *Negro Genius,* published the same year, was an inspired work that drew on Africa but was also uniquely American. Negro genius is lyrical, he said: "The blacks are the singers and the seers." In Harlem—"the first concentration in history," claimed Locke, "of so many diverse elements of Negro life"—these new visions flourished in the Harlem Renaissance.

Langston Hughes "didn't want to do anything but live in Harlem." His poetry, distinguished by sharp wit and insightful social commentary, earned international fame. Paul Robeson's commanding presence and powerful singing voice launched an international career in the theater. In her fiction, Zora Neale Hurston interwove the dialect of black southerners with the language of a collegiate scholar. Other writers such as Claude McKay, Charles Waddell Chesnutt, and Jean Tomer celebrated black life and explored a new black racial identity. New opportunities allowed African American women to pursue individual goals. Bessie Coleman performed flight stunts, Lucy Diggs Slowe won a tennis championship, and singer Marian Anderson won voice competitions.

The Jazz Age

Some historians consider jazz the only art form to have originated in America. It was born of a blend of European and African percussion, horn, and piano melodies, encompassing forms from spirituals to the blues, from the percussion of marching band rhythms to the asymmetry of ragtime. Jazz is always in motion, always morphing from something familiar to something new. Introduced to the French during World War I by black horn player James Reese, jazz won international acclaim. Louis Armstrong's trumpet exemplified the Chicago style. Bessie Smith's hit recordings on radio earned her a fortune. Ethel Waters sang the "St. Louis Blues."

Political Goals and Setbacks in the 1920s

Although cities opened new opportunities for black people, wage disparities between black and white workers persisted, and as the robust economy of the early 1920s faded, the wage discrepancy widened. Thus it is not surprising that the Communist Party, with its calls for social equality and class solidarity, began to gain ground among black working people. Although national politicians sought support from the increasingly urban black voting block, it rarely translated into support for black Americans. No president during the 1920s advocated passage of the Dyer anti-lynching bill. Still, the concentration of black voters in northern cities was beginning to bring political power, and in 1928 Republican Oscar de Priest won election to the U.S. House of Representatives, the first black man in Congress since 1901.

LEARNING OBJECTIVES

Students should be able to
- describe the triumphs and tribulations of black soldiers in World War I.
- discuss the factors leading to the migration of southern blacks within the United States.
- explain the ideas of the black nationalist movement.
- discuss the importance of the Harlem Renaissance.

IDENTIFICATIONS

Explain the significance of each of the following:

1. Thomas Edward Jones

2. 24th Infantry

3. Newton Baker

4. Emmett J. Scott

5. 369th Infantry

6. 371st Infantry

7. 368th Infantry

8. Claude McKay

9. The Great Migration

10. Black Towns

11. East St. Louis Riot

12. Tulsa, Oklahoma Riot

13. Dyer Anti-lynching Bill

14. KKK

15. A. Philip Randolph

16. Brotherhood of Sleeping Car Porters

17. UNIA

18. Marcus Garvey

19. Pan African Conferences

20. NAACP

21. Charles Houston

22. Buck Franklin

23. Lift Every Voice and Sing

24. Charles S. Johnson

25. Alaine Locke

26. New Negro

27. Harlem Renaissance

28. Benjamin Brawley

29. Charles Chesnut

30. Langston Hughes

31. Paul Robeson

32. Zora Neale Hurston

33. Bessie Coleman

34. Lucy Slowe

35. Marian Anderson

36. Amy Ashwood Garvey

37. Violette Anderson

38. Negro History Week

39. Eugene O'Neill

40. Jazz

41. Louis Armstrong

42. James Europe

43. Bessie Smith

44. Ethel Waters

45. Billie Holiday

46. Oscar DePriest

MULTIPLE CHOICE

1. Which of the following best describes the attitude of both national political parties towards African Americans during the 1920s?
   A. They both were very interested in ending segregation and improving conditions.
   B. They both encouraged African Americans to join the Communist Party.
   C. They both gave lip service to African Americans but little else.
   D. They both adopted an agenda which included African Americans.

2. Jazz music served as a great unifier of people. Why was Jazz music so special to Americans?
   A. Jazz music was started by Whites but became popular amongst African Americans.
   B. Jazz was a uniquely American invention.
   C. Jazz music was brought to America by the French after World War II.
   D. Jazz music helped to segregate the music industry in the U.S.

3. During the Harlem Renaissance, African American writers, artists, and poets were producing material to satisfy
   A. White professionals and intellectuals who could judge good work.
   B. African American intellectuals who could approve their work.
   C. the European arts community which generally set world standards.
   D. their individual artistic sensibilities.

4. African American women distinguished themselves during this period in the entertainment world. All of the following are examples of success stories EXCEPT
   A. Marian Anderson.
   B. Ethel Waters.
   C. Billie Holiday.
   D. Alice Dunbar Nelson.

5.	Which of the following best describes the role African American soldiers played in World War I?
	A.	African Americans served mainly as laborers and did not participate in combat.
	B.	African American soldiers dishonored their race and units by constantly running when the battle became intense.
	C.	African American soldiers performed their duties honorably despite the prevalence of racism.
	D.	African American soldiers refused to participate in the war effort because of racism.

6.	Which of the following best describes the impact of Marcus Garvey on African Americans?
	A.	Garvey had a tremendous impact on ordinary African Americans.
	B.	Garvey had limited influence except amongst upper-class African Americans.
	C.	Garvey made African Americans ashamed of themselves and their lack of progress.
	D.	Marcus Garvey encouraged African Americans to integrate into American society.

7.	All of the following are true of the UNIA EXCEPT that it:
	A.	was a worldwide organization.
	B.	was very successful at collecting money and opening businesses.
	C.	organized several large parades to celebrate Blackness.
	D.	eventually merged with the NAACP.

8.	W.E.B. Du Bois and Marcus Garvey differed over what was best for Africa. Which of the following best summarizes their differences?
	A.	Marcus Garvey did not believe that African Americans were Africans.
	B.	Marcus Garvey blacks from the Western Hemisphere to establish an independent nation in Africa.
	C.	Du Bois wanted to bring Whites to Africa to foster integration.
	D.	Du Bois wanted the U.S. government to run African affairs.

9.	The NAACP was able to challenge all of the following during the 1920s EXCEPT
	A.	residential segregation.
	B.	unfair hearings in courtrooms.
	C.	the right to participate in primaries.
	D.	school segregation.

10.	All of the following are true statements concerning the economic situation for African Americans during the 1920s EXCEPT:
	A.	African Americans got new opportunities in industry.
	B.	African American women entered the workforce in larger numbers.
	C.	Most barriers to African American advancement were removed.
	D.	African Americans received better jobs with higher wages, but they still faced discrimination.

11. All of the following statements describe the White reaction to African American migration to urban areas <u>EXCEPT</u>:
    A. Whites confined African Americans to designated parts of the city.
    B. Most cities instituted neighborhood integration.
    C. There were several violent riots, which resulted in the loss of life and property.
    D. There were increases in African American community-based activities.

12. African Americans established an intellectual legacy during the 1920s. All of the following are African Americans who distinguished themselves <u>EXCEPT</u>
    A. Langston Hughes.
    B. Jesse B. Semple.
    C. Paul Robeson.
    D. Zora Neale Hurston.

13. Bessie Smith became one of the most influential African Americans of the 1920s earning in excess of $2,500 a week. What was her talent?
    A. She was a poet.
    B. She was a movie star.
    C. She was an artist.
    D. She was a singer.

14. Joe King Oliver is most closely associated with the formation of
    A. jazz music.
    B. housing in Harlem.
    C. auto industry.
    D. organized crime.

15. In 1928 Africans scored a political victory when
    A. they received a cabinet position in the Coolidge administration.
    B. Oscar DePriest was elected to Congress from Chicago.
    C. they won the mayoral race in East St. Louis, Missouri.
    D. the Leonidas Dyer's amendment passed in Congress, outlawing lynching.

THOUGHT QUESTIONS

1. Using the Josephine Baker document, what can we learn about Whites' interest in African Americans during the 1920s?

2. During the Harlem Renaissance, African American intellectuals of the 1920s tried to produce art that satisfied their individual taste. Why was that important and different from other periods?

3. How does African American participation in the First World War demonstrate their desire to earn respect and equal treatment?

4. How did the Great Migration transform America's race problem from a regional to a national problem?

5. Why was the Marcus Garvey movement so important for ordinary African Americans?

6. How does "A. Philip Randolph's Demands a New Ministry" fit into the notion of a New Negro?

7. How does the NAACP's attack on segregation and racism demonstrate a changed attitude within the African American community?

ANSWER KEY MULTIPLE CHOICE QUESTIONS

1. C
2. B
3. D
4. D
5. C
6. A
7. D
8. B
9. D
10. C
11. B
12. B
13. D
14. A
15. B

CHAPTER 15 *The New Politics of the Great Depression*

CHAPTER SUMMARY

Opening Vignette: The Scottsboro Boys

In March 1931, nine black youths were arrested in Scottsboro, Alabama, following a fistfight with white youths on a train. Rather than assault, to their surprise they were charged with raping two white women who were also on the train. In previous years, they might have been promptly lynched. The nation was in the midst of economic catastrophe; seizing an opportunity to unite workers against "the Scottsboro Frame-Up," the Communist Party took up their cause, spurring various forms of black militancy and catalyzing debates about the future of black politics.

African Americans in Desperate Times

All Americans were profoundly affected by the Great Depression, but black Americans experienced added hardships due to racial discrimination. Unemployment reached 25 percent, but black unemployment was twice that in many cities. Intensified competition for urban jobs disadvantaged black people, but, with floods, boll weevil infestations, and falling cotton prices, the conditions for rural black southerners were more dire.

In this crisis, Communist appeals proved effective. In the late 1920s the party had established the League of Struggle for Negro Rights to combat racial discrimination as well as economic oppression. Now its Scottsboro campaign attracted new members—to the dismay of NAACP leaders. Birmingham laborer Angelo Herndon enthusiastically joined the Scottsboro effort and became a Communist organizer; poet Langston Hughes agreed to serve as president of the league. Hughes risked his career, but the risks for black workers like Herndon were more serious. The threat of violence loomed large in Alabama, where the Sharecroppers Union was campaigning for sharecropper rights. Bloody clashes followed, and when Herndon was arrested in an Atlanta protest, his case, too, became a rallying point for Communists. As the 1932 election approached, the Communist Party attempted to strengthen black support by running a black vice presidential candidate, James Ford. Most black people still voted Republican, but Democrat Franklin D. Roosevelt won the presidency.

Black Militancy

For the NAACP, the upsurge of Communist agitation and the launching of Roosevelt's New Deal posed a dilemma. Walter White, NAACP head, withdrew the organization from the controversial Scottsboro case, but W.E.B. Du Bois, who agreed with White that the Communists were exploiting the case, thought the NAACP had to address economic inequality to "solve the larger Negro problem." Du Bois also questioned the organization's single-minded devotion to integrationist policies. Following a second Amenia Conference at which brash young intellectuals such as Ralph Bunche, Charles Hamilton Houston, and E. Franklin Frazier promoted interracial efforts to unionize industrial workers, and following several *Crisis* articles that challenged the NAACP's approach, Du Bois resigned from the organization he had helped to found. At age sixty-six, he could have retired. Instead, he accepted John Hope's invitation to teach at Atlanta University and began a productive period of study, scholarship, and activism. It seemed that White had prevailed over Du Bois, but Du Bois's criticisms, the dire conditions of the Depression, and new developments in the Scottsboro case finally forced a shift in the NAACP's direction. Under Houston, a brilliant lawyer, it launched a new campaign against school desegregation. Houston and the lawyers he recruited, including Thurgood Marshall and William Hastie, sought cases that would expose obvious racial inequities in public education and force states to undertake the expensive, impractical task of living up to the "separate but equal" standard of *Plessy.* In 1938, in *Missouri ex rel. v. Canada,* the Supreme Court agreed that Missouri must make legal training available to qualified applicants regardless of race. Previously focused on its unsuccessful anti-lynching campaign, the NAACP now set out to secure civil rights for African Americans.

Many African Americans rejected the NAACP's goal of integration. The Depression sparked both leftist radicalism and black nationalism. In Detroit, former Garveyite Elijah Poole joined the Nation of Islam and changed his name to Elijah Muhammad. Historian Carter G. Woodson argued that African Americans had to rely on their own resources. And a small group of college-educated clergy, including Martin Luther King Sr. in Atlanta and Adam Clayton Powell Sr. in Harlem, advocated a social gospel version of Christianity to achieve economic equality and social justice. Cult preacher Father Divine appealed to black and white followers with his Peace Missions and Peace Kitchens. At Howard, a new intellectual elite supported Scottsboro efforts, launched boycotts against businesses discriminating against black workers, and championed Ethiopia following its invasion by Italy. Bunche, in particular, took an international view, studying the stirrings of anticolonialism in Africa and warning of the rise of fascism in Europe. The success of Roosevelt's New Deal confirmed their sense that America could solve its economic problems without revolution, and many accepted positions in New Deal agencies.

A New Deal for African Americans?

The most influential African American in the New Deal was Mary McLeod Bethune, revered educator and founder of the National Council of Negro Women. Though reluctant to leave Bethune-Cookman College, she recognized the significance a position in the National Youth Administration would have for "Negro women coming after me, filling positions of high trust and strategic importance." Her ability to collaborate with people who held differing views served her well as a New Dealer. She realized that Roosevelt was no racial liberal, but she urged the president to tackle racial discrimination even as she defended him against his harshest black critics. Her friendship with Eleanor Roosevelt also allowed her to influence the president. With Robert Weaver, another "advisor for Negro affairs" in the New Deal, she assembled the Black Cabinet, giving visibility to black participation in the Roosevelt administration.

Weaver and Hastie, an assistant solicitor in the Interior Department, and others were often critical of the New Deal's failings: a failure to pass anti-lynching legislation, discrimination in the distribution of relief payments, exclusion of the two largest categories of black workers (agricultural laborers and domestic servants) from minimum-wage rules, overtime rules, and Social Security coverage. Critiques of the New Deal were expressed in the National Negro Congress, founded by black labor leader A. Philip Randolph to achieve more far-reaching social change. But Roosevelt successfully countered criticism though his savvy appointments of African Americans, and more and more blacks concluded that the New Deal, despite its limitations, was the best available political option. For many, jobs and training through the NYA and the Works Progress Administration (WPA) provided the best wages they ever received. Moreover, new federal protections to unions also benefited African Americans. In 1936, they voted Democratic overwhelmingly, abandoning the party of Lincoln and joining the northern liberal-labor coalition that competed with southern conservatives for control of the party.

Black Artists and the Cultural Mainstream

WPA projects gave many black unemployed artists, actors, musicians, and writers their first opportunity to earn a living while developing their talent. Working for the Writers' Project in Chicago, Margaret Walker met Richard Wright. The exchange such projects fostered, she recognized, helped end "the long isolation of the Negro artist." Others who received crucial support included Ralph Ellison, Zora Neale Hurston, Aaron Douglas, Jacob Lawrence, and Shirley Graham.

Paul Robeson's fame brought success not dependent on federal programs, and he could accept the risks that came with leftist political ties. In an era when black actors were confined to comic bit roles, Robeson resolved to accept only parts that portrayed blacks in a positive light. He sustained his career as a singer even as a gulf opened between his preference for traditional African American music, such as slave spirituals, and the commercially popular music of the day. For him, the entry of American Americans into the nation's cultural mainstream represented a loss of cultural integrity. While some southern blues singers, such as Leadbelly and Josh White, maintained the old traditions, many African Americans welcomed the new trends. The appeal of swing bands led by Duke Ellington and Cab Calloway transcended racial lines. When singer Marian Anderson was denied permission to perform at Constitution Hall, Eleanor Roosevelt arranged for a concert at the Lincoln Memorial that drew 75,000.

Richard Wright exemplifies the decline of leftist radicalism and his *Native Son* a new writing based not on political aims or on pleasing white audiences but on conveying the complexities of American race relations. A southerner who migrated to Chicago, Wright had joined the Communist Party but his political views had continued to evolve. In the late 1930s, he lost patience with the party's endless ideological bickering and pressures for ideological conformity and began to openly criticize Communist propaganda. In Bigger Thomas, the protagonist of his best-selling novel, he echoed Scottsboro's story of class and racial oppression, but he made Thomas guilty, then examined the crime as resulting from a series of tragic misunderstandings rooted in racial and class differences.

LEARNING OBJECTIVES

Students will be able to
- describe how the Great Depression altered American politics for blacks.
- identify the political ideas of the Communist Party and the NAACP.
- discuss how the New Deal both benefited and failed African Americans.
- describe the work of black artists, writers, and musicians during the 1930s.
- explain how the mobilization for WWII impacted African Americans.

IDENTIFICATIONS

Explain the significance of each of the following:

1. Scottsboro Boys

2. Communist Party

3. Angelo Herndon

4. William Patterson

5. Haywood Patterson

6. International Labor Defense (ILD)

7. Sharecroppers Union

8. Benjamin J. Davis

9. Franklin D. Roosevelt

10. New Deal

11. Walter White

12. W.E.B. Du Bois

13. Amenia Conference

14. Charles Houston

15. Thurgood Marshall

16. *Missouri ex el v. Canada*

17. Elijah Muhammad

18. Ethiopian World Federation Council

19. Carter G. Woodson

20. Martin Luther King, Sr.

21. Adam Clayton Powell, Jr.

22. Father Divine

23. Mary McLeod Bethune

24. Robert Weaver

25. William Hastie

26. Black Cabinet

27. National Conference on the Problems of the Negro

28. A. Philip Randolph

29. Margaret Walker

30. Richard Wright

31. Paul Robeson

32. Hattie McDaniel

33. Billie Holiday

34. Thomas Dorsey

35. Marian Anderson

36. *Native Son*

MULTIPLE CHOICE

1. The Scottsboro Boys were accused of
    A. murder.
    B. rape.
    C. being Communists.
    D. illegally riding on trains.

2. The Scottsboro Boys were defended in their appeal by which organization?
    A. Communist Party
    B. Urban League
    C. Anti-Defamation League
    D. NACW

3. The most influential African American working for the Roosevelt administration was
    A. Judge William Hastie.
    B. Robert Weaver.
    C. Ralph Bunche.
    D. Mary McLeod Bethune.

4.   Big city African American ministers became more socially and politically active during the 1930s. All of the following were African American religious leaders EXCEPT
        A. Martin Luther King, Sr.
        B. Father Divine.
        C. Adam Clayton Powell.
        D. Billy Sunday.

5.   The economic chaos of the 1930s posed a serious challenge to the NAACP. What was the major complaint about the organization?
        A. It had no economic program to go along with its social program.
        B. There were not enough people from the older generation in the organization.
        C. The NAACP was giving away too much money that should have been spent elsewhere.
        D. The NAACP could no longer attract White support.

6.   Franklin Roosevelt's New Deal program changed the African American political landscape by
        A. bringing African Americans into his cabinet.
        B. convincing a majority of African Americans to vote for the Democrats.
        C. attracting rural voters to the Democratic Party.
        D. outlawing segregation in the south.

7.   Which of the following best characterizes Roosevelt's attitude towards African American rights?
        A. He was willing to expend a lot of political capital on civil rights.
        B. Roosevelt aggressively pushed for his New Deal programs being administered fairly.
        C. Roosevelt designed specific programs to help African Americans.
        D. Roosevelt refused to challenge southerners over issues of civil rights.

8.   The Amenia Conference was designed to bring younger intellectuals into the NAACP. All of the following attended EXCEPT
        A. Ralph Bunche.
        B. E. Franklin Frazier.
        C. Charles Houston.
        D. .Thurgood Marshall.

9.   During the 1930s several prominent African Americans explored joining the Communist Party. The Communist party did all of the following EXCEPT:
        A. They supported complete racial equality.
        B. They ran an African American for vice president.
        C. They defended the Scottsboro Boys.
        D. They successfully integrated several unions.

10. One of the most articulate proponents of African American achievements was Carter G. Woodson. He did all of the following EXCEPT

    A. write the book *The Mis-Education of the Negro.*
    B. start the celebration of Negro History Week.
    C. create the Association for the Study of Negro Life and History.
    D. write the first African American history book.

11. Howard University served as the African American intellectual capital. All of the following individuals taught there EXCEPT

    A. Charles Hamilton Houston.
    B. Alaine Locke.
    C. Charles Drew.
    D. W.E.B. Du Bois.

12. One of the most important New Deal programs was the WPA. How did this organization help African American intellectuals?

    A. It offered many unemployed artists, actors, musicians and writers an opportunity to earn a living using their talents.
    B. It was one of the few governmental programs administered by African Americans.
    C. It was the only New Deal program that provided direct aid to suffering people.
    D. It was the only New Deal program specifically developed to help Blacks.

13. One of the major complaints about the New Deal programs from African Americans was that

    A. there was racial bias in the distribution of New Deal funds.
    B. there were no programs that aided African Americans.
    C. African Americans did not get any of the benefits from the programs.
    D. no African Americans were hired in administrative positions.

14. One of the most significant African American women of the 1930s was Mary McLeod Bethune. She did all of the following EXCEPT

    A. run the Negro Division of the National Youth Administration.
    B. found the school Bethune Cookman in Florida.
    C. serve as president of the National Association of Colored Women.
    D. run unsuccessfully for a position in the U.S. Congress.

15. African Americans made significant advances in the arts and entertainment fields during the 1930s. All of the following individuals are examples of African American success stories EXCEPT:

    A. Paul Robeson.
    B. Louis Armstrong.
    C. Richard Wright.
    D. John Coltrane.

THOUGHT QUESTIONS

1. Describe how the Elle Baker and Marvel Cooke article paints a grim picture of employment opportunities during the depression.

2. Develop an argument supporting the idea that the actions of the Alabama courts during the Scottsboro case show that the state had made progress on racial issues.

3. Explain the significance of Charles Hamilton Houston in dismantling the Jim Crow system.

4. How much weight did Adam Clayton Powell's threats of a boycott against New York businesses have?

5. Based on what T. Arnold Hill says and the accompanying chart, why do the effects of the depression hit African American workers harder than Whites?

6. Compare and contrast the problems associated with teaching in rural and urban African Americans schools during the 1930s.

ANSWER KEY MULTIPLE CHOICE QUESTIONS

1. B.
2. A
3. D
4. D
5. A
6. B
7. D
8. D
9. D
10. D
11. D
12. A
13. A
14. D
15. D

CHAPTER 16 *Fighting Fascism Abroad and Racism at Home*

CHAPTER SUMMARY

Opening Vignette: A. Philip Randolph Challenges President Roosevelt

After World War II began in Europe and America's defense industries expanded to meet war demands, A. Philip Randolph urged President Franklin D. Roosevelt to end racial discrimination in these industries and in the military. When Roosevelt took no action, Randolph planned a march on Washington that became a widespread political movement. As a direct result of this threat, Roosevelt issued Executive Order 8802, ending discrimination in defense industries.

African Americans in the Armed Forces

Dorie Miller, mess attendant second class, was awarded the Navy Cross for bravery at Pearl Harbor, but his heroism did little to open opportunities for black sailors, who were limited to noncombat positions in the Navy. His story is emblematic of the experience of African Americans in the U.S. Armed Forces in World War II: even as they contributed to the war against fascism and Adolf Hitler's racial doctrines, they faced racism in their own country and ranks. Despite Randolph's success in defense industries, black soldiers in the military continued to be assigned to segregated units and menial roles.

To court black voters, in 1940 Roosevelt had asked William H. Hastie, dean of Howard University's law school, to serve as a civilian advisor on racial issues. Though he could not change the military's racial policies, Hastie was well placed to monitor black discontent. His office heard from black soldiers about acts of violence against them as well as discrimination in promotion and training. His pleas ignored, Hastie resigned, admired by black Americans and briefly embarrassing the Roosevelt administration.

Early in 1942 the *Pittsburgh Courier* launched the "Double-V Campaign," which called for victory of the Axis on the battlefront and victory over racial prejudice on the home front. Seeking to push the nation to live up to its historic democratic principles and those expressed in the Atlantic Charter, gains came only with struggle. Despite Roosevelt's executive order, black employment in defense industries rose only when labor shortages became acute. And black soldiers were placed in combat only after casualties mounted, in 1944. The combat successes of the Tuskegee Airmen were also persuasive.

Racial Issues on the Home Front

In March 1940, Pauli Murray applied the Gandhian technique of "nonviolent resistance coupled with good will" when she was jailed for violating Virginia's bus segregation laws. She lost her legal case but became convinced of the power of creative nonviolence. As a student at Howard's law school, she joined the pacifist Fellowship of Reconciliation and helped organize a sit-down protest at a segregated Washington restaurant. But she also experienced gender discrimination, which she quickly labeled Jane Crow. Though an excellent student who argued for a frontal assault on the constitutionality of segregation per se (a strategy later adopted by the NAACP), she was denied admission to a Harvard master's program because she was a woman. Enrolling at the University of California's law school, she met international students who helped her see civil rights in the context of human rights. Other FOR activists, such as James Farmer and pacifist Bayard Rustin, were developing similar ideas, and Farmer formed the Congress of Racial Equality. Murray's hopes to join the NAACP's legal team were disappointed, but the team continued its successes: *Smith v. Allwright* outlawed "white primaries," and *Shelley v. Kraemer* ruled that racially restrictive housing covenants were unenforceable.

In 1943, Murray was in Harlem one day after a riot that made the streets look like a "bombed-out war zone." Earlier in the year, there had been a violent clash in Detroit that had also taken lives and property. Competition for jobs and discrimination in housing made fistfights and rumors flashpoints for black insurrection. "These riots had to come," was her conclusion.

Postwar Dilemmas

Civil rights gains during the war were limited: the military was still largely segregated, and the Fair Employment Practices Committee, established by Roosevelt's executive order on defense industries, had no enforcement power and was not scheduled to continue. Roosevelt's death left more uncertainties, as Truman's response to civil rights issues was unknown. Race relations were better understood thanks to the work of social scientists, including Gunnar Myrdal's *An American Dilemma,* as well as landmark studies by St. Clair Drake, Horace Cayton, Robert Weaver, and John Hope Franklin. But postwar tensions, especially over jobs for returning veterans, indicated that enlightened scholarship was not enough. A riot erupted in Columbia, Tennessee, and fifty-six black Americans were killed in episodes of racial violence all over the country.

For Ralph Bunche, State Department advisor and delegate to the United Nations founding conference, the civil rights struggle was linked to decolonization movements, but the Truman administration was reluctant to pressure Britain and France on these issues and made sure the UN could not intervene in domestic matters, thus protecting segregation within the United States. Yet Truman was aware that segregation damaged U.S. credibility as the leader of democratic nations now engaged in a new contest against the Soviet Union—the Cold War.

Cold War Split in African American Politics

As the Cold War intensified, any criticism of America was liable to charges of being "communist inspired." The result was a major division in African American politics. Langston Hughes and Richard Wright, once associated with Communist organizations, now distanced themselves. Thurgood Marshall and Walter White carefully aligned the NAACP with the anticommunism and the Truman administration.

But W.E.B. Du Bois and Paul Robeson doubted Truman would act for civil rights. Du Bois, once again with the NAACP, now as head of the research office, drafted *An Appeal to the World,* aiming to bring the issue of U.S. racial discrimination before the UN Human Rights Commission. When the Soviet Union agreed to sponsor it, the appeal caused a serious rift within the NAACP. Eleanor Roosevelt threatened to resign from the board, but White removed Du Bois instead. Du Bois moved on to the Council on African Affairs, which Robeson had helped to found to aid national liberation struggles in Africa. Now Robeson emerged as the most energetic and popular proponent of an African American leftist perspective, denouncing lynching, pointing to the irony of Nazi war crimes trials while America ignored its own moral crimes, and challenging Truman to act. By the time Truman's Civil Rights Commission issued its report *To Secure These Rights* and Truman announced support for its recommendations, Robeson was already under investigation by the House Committee on Un-American Activities.

The 1948 presidential campaign further split black political leadership. Du Bois and Robeson supported Henry Wallace, the Progressive Party candidate. Truman recruited Hastie to campaign on his behalf in black communities. Then Randolph mounted a new effort to desegregate the armed forces, joining with Rustin to encourage black draft resistance. After southern Democrats led by Strom Thurmond left the Democratic Party to form the States' Rights Party, Truman had a freer hand on civil rights and issued executive orders banning racial discrimination in federal employment and the armed forces. His razor-thin victory in the election was owing to black support.

In the aftermath of Wallace's overwhelming defeat, the ideological boundaries of African American politics narrowed. As pressures for political conformity increased, the internationalism of Du Bois and Robeson was obscured by their Communist ties. Nor could non-Communists such as Randolph and Rustin thrive in the Cold War political climate. But the NAACP moved to the forefront, forging ties with liberal politicians, labor unions, and Jewish organizations, and achieving highly visible legal victories that forced states to make equal educational facilities available to black students in law and graduate schools. Marshall's Legal Defense and Education Fund not only undermined the legal foundations of the separate-but-equal doctrine, but also provided a substitute for mass protest.

Racial Dimensions of Postwar Culture

Even as Robeson continued to promote traditional African American musical forms, many black artists and performers pursued success within the constraints of the capitalist system and Cold War liberalism that he denounced. Swing and the big band sound gave way to an experimental jazz style known as bebop, but most African Americans were listening to "race music"—rhythm and blues—now promoted by black-owned radio stations and DJs. In Hollywood, opportunities expanded for black actors willing to accept the limited roles offered them. But the most surprising development came in sports: Jackie Robinson's famous breaking of the color bar in major league baseball. Robinson had challenged bus segregation in the military during World War II, but he agreed to suppress aggression in the desegregation experiment engineered by Brooklyn Dodgers owner Branch Rickey. Many Americans saw him as a hero, but he was also a model for gradual or token racial reform that did not alter African American lives.

LEARNING OBJECTIVES

Students should be able to
- discuss how blacks fought racism during World War II.
- explain the racist backlash against the gains made by African Americans.
- describe the new tactics used by black activists.
- discuss the goals of various African American political groups.
- analyze the effect of the Cold War on African American politics.

IDENTIFICATIONS

Explain the significance of each of the following:

1. A. Philip Randolph

2. Dorie Miller

3. William Hastie

4. Benjamin O. Davis, Sr.

5. Benjamin O. Davis, Jr.

6. Double V. Campaign

7. Jackie Robinson

8. Lena Horne

9. Port Chicago Incident

10. Tuskegee Airmen

11. Freeman Airfield Incident

12. Pauli Murray

13. Fellowship of Reconciliation FOR

14. James Farmer

15. Committee on Racial Equality

16. Bayard Rustin

17. "Sitdowns"

18. Detroit Riots

19. Thurgood Marshall

20. Lonnie Smith

21. Gunnar Myrdal

22. Macio Snipes

23. Ralph Bunche

24. UN Commission on Human Rights

25. Paul Robeson

26. Executive Orders 9980 and 9981

27. NAACP

28. Adam Clayton Powell, Jr.

29. Legal Defense and Education Fund

30. Constance Baker Motley

31. Bebop

32. Alfred Bernard Learner

33. Canada Lee

34. Jackie Robinson

MULTIPLE CHOICE

1. The major difference between Jackie Robinson and Paul Robeson was
    A. Jackie Robinson never played football; he was a one-sport athlete.
    B. Paul Robeson never went to college; he was drafted straight out of high school.
    C. Paul Robeson allied himself with the Communist Party to fight racism.
    D. Jackie Robinson absolutely refused to participate in civil rights activities.

2. Outspoken African Americans were often silenced by accusations of having communist ties. Which of the following was a successful African American Hollywood actor blacklisted during the 1950s for alleged communists ties?
    A. Lena Horne
    B. Bill Robinson
    C. Eddie Robinson
    D. Canada Lee

3. The revolt of young African American musicians like Charlie Parker, Dizzy Gillespie, and Theolonius Monk was called
    A. swing.
    B. big band.
    C. bebop.
    D. pop.

4. The NAACP launched a nationwide assault on segregation during the 1940s and 1950s. Who was the chief NAACP attorney for most of these cases?
    A. Charles Hamilton Houston
    B. Thurgood Marshall
    C. Spottswood Robinson
    D. Robert Lee Carter

5. Harry Truman won the 1948 election mainly as a result of
    A. attracting the votes of the left wing.
    B. winning the votes of Urban Blacks.
    C. defeating Strom Thurman in the South.
    D. uniting the Democratic Party.

6. The Cold War politics split the African American community. Which of the following did not denounce communism during the 1940s and 1950s?
    A. A. Philip Randolph
    B. Thurgood Marshall
    C. Walter White
    D. W.E.B. Dubois

7. African Americans were very disappointed in the UN when it was finally organized because
    A. they did not build the headquarters in Harlem.
    B. no African Americans were invited to participate in the organizing sessions.
    C. the UN Commission on Human Rights refused to get involved in domestic issues.
    D. the UN refused to recognize any African nation's independence.

8. Which of the following best describes the attitude of ordinary white Americans towards black Americans during the Post-War period?
    A. They continued to believe that African Americans should hold a second-class status.
    B. They favored the complete integration of society.
    C. They supported the expulsion of African Americans from the U.S.
    D. The people supported civil rights, but the government did not.

9. One of the most unrecognized figures in African American history was Pauli Murray. Murray did all of the following EXCEPT
    A. work as an attorney for the NAACP Legal Defense and Education Fund.
    B. act as the first African American deputy attorney general of California.
    C. participate in early sit-down strikes lead by student protestors.
    D. graduate from Howard law School and outline a strategy for attacking segregation.

10. One of the most decorated group of pilots was the Tuskegee Airmen. What did White bomber crews call these fighters?
    A. The Buffalo soldiers of the air
    B. The Black Eagle Fighters
    C. The "Red-Tailed Angels"
    D. The Flying Black Knights

11. African Americans were divided on the war issue in the early 1940s. They organized a campaign to wipe out both international fascism and domestic racism. This protest was referred to as
    A. the "Double V" Campaign.
    B. the Down With Racism Campaign.
    C. the We Too Are America Campaign.
    D. the World Peace Campaign.

12. The first American Hero of World War II was
    A. Thomas Dewey.
    B. Dorie Miller.
    C. William Hastie.
    D. Benjamin O. Davis.

13. Which of the following best describes President Roosevelt's attitude towards African Americans during the Second World War?
    A. Roosevelt wanted to use the war to desegregate American society.
    B. Roosevelt ignored Black demands because he wanted to do nothing to upset Whites during the war.
    C. Roosevelt was very proactive and did as much as possible for African Americans.
    D. Roosevelt attempted to build an integrated war effort.

14. A. Philip Randolph used a threat of a march on Washington to force President Roosevelt to issue Executive Order 8802. What did this executive order do?
    A. It integrated the military.
    B. It opened Officer's Training Schools for Blacks.
    C. It ended discrimination in employment in the defense industry.
    D. It appointed a National Director of Civil Rights to ensure fair treatment.

15.   President Harry Truman conducted a study on civil rights in America called *To Secure these Rights* which resulted in Executive Orders 9980 and 9981. What two rights came from these changes?
   A. Integration of the military and an end to discrimination in federal jobs
   B. An end to discrimination in federal jobs and the outlawing of lynching
   C. Integration of the military and outlawing of lynching
   D. Outlawing of lynching and creation of a Federal Employments Practices Commission

THOUGHT QUESTIONS

1. Based upon the flyer distributed by A. Philip Randolph, describe why was it so important that African Americans join the March on Washington, DC.

2. Explain the frustrations described by those interviewed by Pauli Murray during the 1943 Harlem riot. What did the rioters hope to accomplish?

3. Discuss how successful Walter White is in transforming the African American struggle for civil rights into an international struggle for human rights.

4. Describe the ideal relationship between the Western world and the Third World as outlined by Ralph Bunche in his Nobel Prize acceptance speech.

5. Discuss the attempts by the various parties to entice the African American vote in 1948.

6. Describe how the successes in the sports, entertainment, and intellectual world set the stage for the civil rights movement.

ANSWER KEY MULTIPLE CHOICE QUESTIONS

1. C
2. D
3. C
4. B
5. B
6. D
7. C
8. A
9. A
10. C
11. A
12. B
13. B
14. C
15. A

CHAPTER 17 *Emergence of a Mass Movement Against Jim Crow: The 1950s*

CHAPTER SUMMARY

Opening Vignette: Barbara Johns Leads a Student Strike

In April 1951, student Barbara Johns plotted an assembly at Moton High School in Farmville, Virginia. Telling the teachers to leave, she then told the students that they must strike. Pointing to Moton's inadequate facilities, she asserted, "We will not accept these conditions." Calling on the NAACP, she turned the student strike into an NAACP desegregation case that was combined with *Brown v. Board of Education of Topeka* and, three years later, ended segregation in America's public schools.

The Road to *Brown v. Board of Education of Topeka*

In 1950, NAACP leaders were confident that the end of enforced segregation was in sight. Two suits ended segregation in graduate and professional schools. The Supreme Court's finding in *McLaurin* that racial isolation hindered the education of black students was especially significant. So far, the NAACP's strategy had been to force states, on a case-by-case basis, to live up to the <u>equal</u> side of the separate-but-equal doctrine. Now the time has come, asserted Thurgood Marshall's assistant Robert Lee Carter, to argue that separation itself violated the Fourteenth Amendment's equal protection clause. Marshall was cautious; he had always steered a moderate course.

The key to this new approach was selecting the right case. At first NAACP lawyers focused on *Briggs v. Elliott*, a South Carolina case in which facilities for black students, as in Farmville, were clearly unequal. At the NAACP's request, social psychologist Kenneth Clark and his wife Mamie tested the black children's reactions to black and white dolls. Clark testified in the *Briggs* case that segregation caused black children "to reject themselves and their color" and harmed their development. Meanwhile a Kansas case focused squarely on the constitutionality of segregation. In *Brown v. Board of Education of Topeka*, the facilities were, even the plaintiffs agreed, substantially equal. The Supreme Court said it would hear the two cases in June 1952, then quickly added the Moton High School case and two others.

Clearly the cases folded into *Brown* would be the "big one," and Marshall knew that racial progress and the NAACP's reputation rested on the outcome. In the argument, he kept the focus on the destructive consequences of enforced racial isolation. Although President Dwight Eisenhower had not taken a stand, the Justice Department submitted a friend-of-the-court brief and Chief Justice Earl Warren was determined to make the ruling unanimous. Marshall was in the court when Warren announced, "Separate educational facilities are inherently unequal." Although black leaders hailed the ruling as "a second Emancipation Proclamation," Marshall knew that the fight would now focus on enforcement at the local level.

In Montgomery, Alabama, ministers Vernon Johns (Barbara Johns's outspoken uncle), Ralph Abernathy, and Martin Luther King, Jr., who would soon take over Johns's pulpit, discussed the social gospel's call for justice as well as salvation. Reflecting the simmering discontent felt by many African Americans, King and Abernathy, both in their late twenties, would take the initiative in seeking to transform the legal rights upheld by *Brown* into tangible racial advances. They had grown impatient with the NAACP's strategy of reform through litigation and lobbying. And their congregations included activists capable of sustained struggle, including Jo Ann Robinson, who in May 1954 warned Montgomery's mayor that continued segregation of city buses might produce a boycott.

The Montgomery Bus Boycott and the South Christian Leadership Conference

Thus when NAACP activist Rosa Parks was arrested in December 1955 for refusing to give her bus seat to a white man, Montgomery's African Americans were ready for unified action. "It was then that the ministers decided it was time for them to catch up with the masses," Robinson said. When they formed the Montgomery Improvement Association to extend the one-day boycott, they chose King as their leader. He eloquently linked the Montgomery protest to the broader cause of social justice, working closely with local leaders and strengthening the resolve of the city's black residents. His understanding of Gandhian nonviolence deepened through discussions with Bayard Rustin. King's charismatic leadership attracted nationwide press coverage, but it was the resolve of the black people of Montgomery to withstand intimidation and violence that made the boycott a success. They demonstrated that African Americans, though often poor, could be a powerful force when united. After a year-long protest, the Supreme Court ruled that segregated seating on city buses was unconstitutional.

King now turned the energies of MIA members to new objectives, such as voter registration and the desegregation of educational and recreational facilities. Recognizing the need for a regional organization to sustain the momentum of the Montgomery movement, he and other ministers founded the Southern Christian Leadership Conference. He continually linked the southern black struggle to global politics, and his growing international prominence was evident when African leader Kwame Nkrumah invited him to Ghana's independence celebration in 1957. Two months later, at a Prayer Pilgrimage in Washington, King demanded, "Give us the ballot," and SCLC soon announced a Crusade for Citizenship. But grassroots protests were springing up all over the South, without the necessity of a national leader or organization. In Little Rock, black teenagers once again took the lead in challenging segregation.

The Little Rock Nine

NAACP organizer Daisy Bates had helped select nine students to integrate Little Rock's previously all-white Central High School. The first day of school, Minniejean Brown remembered, was "the most afraid I ever was." An angry mob jeered the students, and the National Guard, called out by Governor Orval Faubus, turned them away. The drama of black teenagers braving mob violence attracted international press coverage, and when the violence continued, Eisenhower nationalized the Arkansas Guard and called in the 101st Airborne, the first time since Reconstruction that a president sent troops into the South to enforce the Fourteenth Amendment.

For the students, getting through the school year was a challenge of its own. "I had no experience, really, with white people," Brown recalled. The target of taunts and hostile acts, she turned over her lunch tray in the cafeteria, deliberately spattering chili over four boys who were harassing her. Eventually expelled, she went to live with the Clarks in New York. The other students completed the school year, and all became heroes and role models for many discontented black youths. It seemed as though federal power had prevailed, but Faubus closed the schools the next year. Public schools in Farmville had also closed rather than desegregate. While white students went to white academies, funded with public money, black students had no schools at all.

African Americans were increasingly impatient with white obstructionism and the pace of civil rights reform. Hired to run the SCLC office in Atlanta, activist Ella Baker did her best to invigorate the organization, but local movements, often involving young people, were developing without much guidance from regional or national groups, or even from adults. In an address to the NAACP in 1956 King had called for greater militancy, but even SCLC had done little to stimulate nonviolent protest movements. Baker was convinced that what was needed was a mass movement and leaders who were less interested in leading than in developing leadership in others.

The Student Sit-In Movement

Transferring to Nashville's Fisk University, Diane Nash felt "stifled" by segregation and "the weakening of American influence abroad as a result of race hatred." But she was impressed by the ideas of James Lawson, a theology student who trained students in Gandhian nonviolent direct action. But before they could put their ideas into practice, four students in Greensboro, North Carolina, sat down at a Woolworth's lunch counter where they were not allowed to eat. The next day about thirty students occupied most of the seats. Quickly students at nearby black colleges adopted this simple tactic that put segregationists on the defensive. When Nash and Nashville students undertook a similar protest, the result was mass arrests. Now students at dozens of colleges demonstrated their eagerness to risk jail in expanding the meaning of the *Brown* decision and speeding the pace of racial change.

Although many students were affiliated with the NAACP, their actions offered an implicit challenge to the cautious strategy of the nation's oldest civil rights group. The NAACP gave public support to the sit-ins but privately questioned their usefulness. King's response was more favorable, but he was reluctant to involve the SCLC in direct action campaigns. Baker welcomed the sit-in movement, however, and proposed a meeting of student sit-in leaders. The result was the Student Nonviolent Coordinating Committee, dedicated to "the philosophical or religious ideal of nonviolence," a statement of purpose drafted by Lawton. Already there was a generational gulf dividing student advocates of civil disobedience and the more cautious leadership of both the SCLC and the NAACP.

LEARNING OBJECTIVES

Students should be able to
- discuss the importance of the *Brown v. Board of Education* decision and its impact on American society.
- explain the new types of civil rights activism that emerged in the 1950s.
- describe how African Americans linked their struggles to those of Africans.
- critique the role that the federal government played in civil rights.
- assess the impact of young people on the direction of civil rights activism.

IDENTIFICATIONS

Explain the significance of each of the following:

1. Barbara Rose Johns

2. Thurgood Marshall

3. Linda Brown

4. Kenneth Clark

5. Brown v. Board of Education Topeka, Kansas

6. John W. Davis

7. Earl Warren

8. Vernon Johns

9. Ralph Abernathy

10. KKK

11. Emmett Till

12. Jo Ann Robinson

13. E.D. Nixon

14. Rosa Parks

15. Septima Clark

16. Montgomery Improvement Association

17. Bayard Rustin

18. Fred Shuttlesworth

19. Southern Christian Leadership Conference

20. Daisy Bates

21. Little Rock Nine

22. Ella Baker

23. Lorraine Hansberry

24. Robert F. Williams

25. Diane Nash

26. James Lawson

27. Sit-ins

28. Student Nonviolent Coordinating Committee

MULTIPLE CHOICE QUESTIONS

1. What steps did Barbara Rose Johns take to actualize her goals of dignity and equality?
   A. She joined the NAACP Youth Council.
   B. She organized a student strike to demand a new and improved school.
   C. She held the first civil rights protest on a public transportation system.
   D. She fought back against those who refused to allow her to vote.

2. Thurgood Marshall and the NAACP made a dramatic step towards equalizing society when they
   A. launched a national movement to equalize schools in America.
   B. filed a lawsuit challenging segregation on public transportation systems.
   C. switched strategies from equalizing schools to ending segregation.
   D. hired the first woman to lead the Legal Defense and Education Fund.

3. The first challenges to the unequal educational policies came from those who wanted to
   A. integrate the graduate programs in the country.
   B. hire African American teachers at White schools.
   C. integrate high school students at Central High School in Littlerock, Arkansas.
   D. integrate the University of Mississippi.

4. In 1956 Rev. C.K. Steele and the Inter-Civic Council gained national attention by
   A. organizing the first successful sit-in drive in America.
   B. leading students at Florida A&M University in a bus boycott.
   C. electing the first African American to local government in Anniston, Alabama.
   D. successfully integrating a church in the south.

5. Which organization did African American ministers form in order to link their civil rights struggle with similar efforts around the world?
   A. Southern Christian Leadership Conference
   B. Black Ministerial Association
   C. The Interfaith Ministerial Alliance
   D. International Ministers' Association

6. Daisy Bates gained international prominence when she
   A. became the first African American student to integrate Alabama's schools.
   B. filed suit to integrate nine Black students into the Littlerock, Arkansas public schools.
   C. organized the Youth division of the NAACP.
   D. ran unsuccessfully for political office in Georgia.

7. President Dwight Eisenhower was forced to intervene in the civil rights struggle when
   A. one of his Black staffers was arrested in Georgia for violating a segregation law.
   B. his pollsters informed him that he was losing popularity amongst northerners.
   C. Governor Faubus of Arkansas defied a Federal court order to integrate schools.
   D. Dr. Martin Luther King, Jr. was arrested in Atlanta, Georgia.

8. Although Rosa Parks is credited with starting the bus boycott, there were others who tried before her. All of the following are people who protested the bus policy EXCEPT
   A. Vernon Johns.
   B. Claudette Colvin.
   C. Mary Louise Smith.
   D. Shirley Chisholm.

9. The Emmitt Till case galvanized the attention of the world and demonstrated the hypocrisy of America's justice department when
   A. the men who committed the crime were convicted and then given very light sentences.
   B. Mississippi's Governor commuted the life sentences given to the men convicted of the crime.
   C. the all-White jury quickly acquitted the men charged with the crime.
   D. no one was ever tried for the crime even though it was clear who participated.

10. In the Brown v. Board of Education case Thurgood Marshall used a different strategy by arguing
   A. segregation in and of itself was psychologically destructive to Blacks.
   B. most Whites supported integration even though they were afraid to admit it.
   C. even though segregation was legal, it was not ethical.
   D. if the courts did not equalize the schools, then black southerners would revolt.

11. Kenneth and Mamie Clark were hired by Thurgood Marshall to demonstrate
   A. the fact that African Americans were capable of learning.
   B. African American girls were just as smart as White boys.
   C. segregation had created a feeling of racial inferiority within Black children.
   D. African American and White children learned the same way.

12. The lawyer who argued the Brown case for the South was one of the most respected jurists in the country. Who argued the case?
   A. Walter Perkins
   B. John W. Davis
   C. William Feeley
   D. William F. Buckley

13. Dr. Martin Luther King developed a strategy which combined the teachings of all of the following EXCEPT
   A. Mahatma Gandhi.
   B. Jesus Christ.
   C. Henry Davis Thoreau.
   D. Buddha.

14. The sit-in movement was begun by
   A. White students in Atlanta, Georgia.
   B. Black Students in Greensboro, North Carolina.
   C. housewives in Montgomery, Alabama.
   D. high school students in Dallas, Texas.

15. The significance of student-led protest activities was that
   A. students learned they could lead protests without adult involvement.
   B. students became more independent refusing to join any organizations.
   C. they forced Martin Luther King, Jr. and others to join their organizations.
   D. students learned how to negotiate with governmental leaders.

THOUGHT QUESTIONS

1. Discuss the forces that drove African Americans to challenge the Jim Crow system after World War II.

2. How did the murder of Emmett Till transform Anne Moody's thoughts and behavior?

3. Describe the process Thurgood Marshall and his NAACP lawyers used to dismantle segregation. Why do you think that their strategy was successful?

4. Even though there had been previous civil rights court successes, why was the Brown decision so important?

5. Explain the successes of Rosa Parks and Martin Luther King. What was so important about what they did?

6. Discuss how Claudette Colvin represented a new generation of African American youth.

7. Describe how the events in Little Rock, Arkansas forced the federal government to join the struggle for African American civil rights at the local level.

8. Discuss how Martin Luther King, Jr.'s strategy of nonviolent resistance inspired a generation of people to stand up and fight for their rights.

ANSWER KEY MULTIPLE CHOICE QUESTIONS

1. B
2. C
3. A
4. B
5. A
6. B
7. C
8. D
9. C
10. A
11. C
12. B
13. D
14. B
15. A

CHAPTER 18 *Marching Toward Freedom, 1960–1966*

CHAPTER SUMMARY

Opening Vignette: Freedom Riders Challenge Segregation

In May 1961, student leader Diane Nash, undeterred by the violence that had halted CORE's freedom rides in the South, arranged for the young people of SNCC to carry on. Continuing violence along the route of the ride and in Montgomery, where Martin Luther King addressed a rally, was restrained only by U.S. marshals and National Guard soldiers. Thus did student activists prod veteran activists James Farmer of CORE and King toward greater militancy and force the intervention of state and federal officials.

Grassroots Struggles in the Deep South

At Mississippi's Parchman Farm, where freedom riders were imprisoned, John Lewis, a recent Nashville seminary graduate, met Howard philosophy major Stokely Carmichael, who questioned the Gandhian principles of the Nashville activists. "He was as different from me as night from day," Lewis recalled, "but for some reason I liked him." Lewis also realized that "we were in for a long, bloody fight." SNCC's strategy was to work with grassroots leaders, teaching nonviolent direct action techniques, but in McComb, Mississippi, voter registration efforts led by Bob Moses encountered intense violence. He doubted the federal government's willingness to protect the rights of southern black people but also realized that voter registration would never succeed unless the federal government and the rest of the nation became aware of conditions in the Deep South. In Albany, Georgia, where SNCC organizers sensed a conflict between their bottom-up organizing strategy and King's top-down leadership style, activists also concluded that they could not overcome segregationist resistance in the south without considerable outside support.

The Nationalization of Civil Rights

In 1963, after SCLC's Birmingham campaign had produced hundreds of arrests, King faced a dilemma: he had to be jailed to sustain the campaign, but jailing would prevent his raising funds needed to sustain the campaign. He chose to be jailed, a move that drew national support. Singer Harry Belafonte raised bail funds, and President Kennedy phoned Coretta Scott King to express concern. King's eloquent theological "Letter from Birmingham City Jail" argued that white resistance to black equality had forced blacks to move outside legal channels and create a crisis rather than wait for change. Now SCLC leaders allowed children to participate in the demonstrations. Violent reactions by police with fire hoses and dogs drew worldwide attention, compelling government intervention by Justice Department negotiators and federal troops. Similar protests in more that one hundred cities demonstrated that the civil rights movement had become national.

Insightful articles by James Baldwin, who had just returned from Europe and was traveling through the South reporting on the struggle, made him an influential spokesperson for the new black militancy. He understood that King was "beleaguered"—caught between "his enemies in the South" and black Americans who were "bitter, disappointed, skeptical"—as he attempted to move beyond the accommodationist role traditionally played by national black leaders such as Booker T. Washington. Baldwin also understood why urban blacks had turned from Christianity toward the racial separatism of the Nation of Islam, and he came to share Malcolm X's skepticism of nonviolence. His *TheFire Next Time* described the increasingly militant mood of black Americans and posed the famous question: "Do I really want to be integrated into a burning house?" While urban black Americans admired the sacrifices of southern civil rights protesters, they also knew that an end to *de jure* segregation in the South would have no effect on the widespread *de facto* segregation in the North.

The challenge to federal authority and the mass protests of Birmingham forced Kennedy to call for civil rights legislation, but whether he would risk other priorities for this legislation was uncertain. To put more pressure on the president, A. Philip Randolph called for a march on Washington, a tactic he had used to wrest concessions from Franklin D. Roosevelt. Though black leaders were far from united on this strategy, the march on August 28, 1963, was the largest civil rights demonstration ever held. Randolph, Bayard Rustin, and other organizers drew support from a wide range of labor and religious groups, and black leaders associated with earlier advances, such as Jackie Robinson and Ralph Bunche, were present. John Lewis, caught between the moderate leaders of the march and the increasingly militant SNCC workers, offered a qualified endorsement of Kennedy's proposed legislation. King's famous "I Have a Dream" speech provided a memorable summation of the themes that had guided previous civil rights efforts. But the March's optimism collapsed within a week when the bombing of a black church in Birmingham killed four little girls. After Kennedy himself was assassinated, the new president Lyndon Johnson committed himself to civil rights reform.

Freedom Summer and the Mississippi Democratic Freedom Party

To draw attention to the violence that had stalled SNCC's voter registration campaign in Mississippi, Bob Moses proposed a project to bring hundreds of white students to the state in the summer of 1964. They would, Moses said, "bring the rest of the country with them." Though Carmichael objected that the students would undermine SNCC's aim to develop self-reliant local black leadership, Moses was right about the publicity, especially after three young people—two of them white college students—disappeared near Philadelphia, Mississippi. The FBI, previously reluctant to protect civil rights workers, now launched a massive search, and Johnson succeeded in getting the Civil Rights Act passed, thus ending segregation in public accommodations. The Summer Project ended with the Mississippi Freedom Democratic Party's demand for seating at the state's delegation to the Democratic National Convention. Despite Fannie Lou Hamer's emotional testimony, Johnson was unwilling to risk losing white southern Democrats, and the convention widened the gulf between veterans of the southern struggle, who felt betrayed, and the liberal Democrats who supported Johnson. Carmichael realized that African Americans could not rely on their "so-called allies," and some SNCC workers concluded that alternatives to liberalism, nonviolence, and interracialism were needed.

Malcolm X and the Freedom Struggle

At a chance meeting in Africa, Lewis heard Malcolm X promote using African nations to push to the United Nations to address American racial issues. Having broken with the Nation of Islam, Malcolm was now seeking to build ties with militant civil rights activists just as SNCC workers were looking to expand their efforts into northern inner-city black communities. In February 1965, Malcolm accepted SNCC's invitation to speak in Selma, where a voting rights campaign was under way, but three weeks later he was assassinated by Nation of Islam members. His death did not end his influence, however, as his advocacy of a positive racial identity and his pan-African perspective coincided with the conclusions many black activists were drawing from their own experiences. Alex Haley's *Autobiography of Malcolm X* extended his ideas to an audience that far exceeded those who heard him speak during his lifetime.

Voting Rights and Violence

In 1965, after Jimmy Lee Jackson was killed during a voting rights demonstration in Marion, Alabama, Nash and her husband James Bevel proposed a protest march from Selma to Montgomery. Through a carefully orchestrated series of events they would draw the nation's attention to brutal forces of repression. SNCC planners resented King as an interloper, especially after King left Selma to preach in his Atlanta church on the morning the marchers set out across Pettus Bridge and were beaten back. Relations between SNCC and SCLC further deteriorated, but a second march finally reached Montgomery. The last major racial protest movement to receive substantial white support, it prompted Johnson to propose, and Congress to pass, the Voting Rights Act.

This landmark decision was part of a series of governmental efforts aimed at transforming civil rights into tangible gains. The Great Society sought to end poverty and unemployment, help poor people with food stamps and educational programs such as Head Start, encourage community action programs, and provide low-rent housing. Though this legislation had a major impact, it was uneven. And shortly after the Voting Rights Act was passed, the Watts section of Los Angeles erupted in a rebellion demonstrating that civil and voting rights laws had done little to relieve the problems of America's cities.

Black Power

Carmichael, skeptical about the Selma march, turned his attention to a new project in Lowndes County, which had a black majority but had no black voters. The project's emblem—a snarling black panther—captured the imagination of SNCC staff wanting to replace interracial alliances and nonviolent principles with independent, black-controlled political institutions. When Carmichael was elected SNCC chair, beating Lewis, an era ended. During a march across Mississippi following the shooting of James Meredith, who had integrated the University of Mississippi, Carmichael introduced the "Black Power" slogan. Galvanizing the marchers, it symbolized a major shift in the freedom struggle and in the African American self-concept. Recognizing its potential for alienating white allies, King was troubled that the Movement was abandoning its earlier ideals.

LEARNING OBJECTIVES

Students should be able to
- explain why the civil rights movement became more militant during the 1960s.
- discuss the successes black activists.
- examine the challenges facing African American leaders.
- outline divisions among black leaders and organizations.

IDENTIFICATIONS

Explain the significance of each of the following:

1. Diane Nash

2. James Farmer

3. John Lewis

4. Freedom Riders

5. SNCC

6. Bob Moses

7. COFO

8. Fannie Lou Hamer

9. Albany Movement

10. Bull Connor

11. Bombingham

12. Letter from Birmingham City Jail

13. James Baldwin

14. Robert Kennedy

15. John F. Kennedy

16. A Philip Randolph

17. Bayard Rustin

18. Mississippi Freedom Democratic Party (MFDP)

19. 1964 Summer Project

20. Civil Rights Act of 1964

21. Malcolm X

22. Muhammad Ali

23. Jimmy Lee Jackson

24. Lyndon B. Johnson

25. Watts Rebellion

26. Lowndes County Freedom Organization (LCFO)

27. Black Panther Party

28. Black Power

29. Stokely Carmichael

30. James Meredith

MULTIPLE CHOICE

1. Why did James Baldwin think that Martin Luther King's role was different from that of Booker T. Washington's and other traditional Black leaders?
    A. King wanted to improve his individual status.
    B. King wanted to move African Americans to full first-class status.
    C. King had an organization behind him.
    D. King was better educated than people like W.E.B. Dubois and Booker T. Washington.

2. John F. Kennedy changed his mind on civil rights after witnessing all of the following EXCEPT:
    A. His brother met with African American leaders in New York City.
    B. Alabama Governor George Wallace barred Black students from integrating the University of Alabama.
    C. The mass protest in Alabama against civil rights.
    D. His African American friend was killed by Klansmen in Mississippi.

3.	There were several groups that opposed the March on Washington for their own reasons. Which of the following is <u>NOT</u> true?
    A. The Kennedy Administration opposed the March because they feared the effect on proposed Civil Rights legislation.
    B. The Nation of Islam opposed the March because they did not support the nonviolent movement.
    C. Federal officials opposed the March for fear that communists would lead organizing efforts.
    D. White southerners opposed the March because they did not want to lose their workers for a day.

4.	The various civil rights organizations often clashed because they had different agendas. This infighting caused civil rights proponents to fail in which campaign?
    A. The Montgomery Movement
    B. The Albany Movement
    C. The St. Augustine Movement
    D. The Detroit Movement

5.	Fred Shuttlesworth the SCLC leader in Birmingham wanted Dr. Martin Luther King, Jr. to come there to deal with all of the following <u>EXCEPT</u>
    A. Police Chief Bull Connor who used violence to enforce segregation.
    B. the high number of bombings which characterized the city of Birmingham.
    C. Governor George Wallace who had dedicated himself to stubborn resistance to integration.
    D. the re-segregation of the city's public bus system.

6.	The Birmingham Movement proved to be one of the most significant landmarks on the Civil Rights trail. All of the following happened during that Movement <u>EXCEPT</u> Martin Luther King, Jr.
    A. wrote his famous letter from the Birmingham jail.
    B. used children as protesters exposing them to violence and abuse.
    C. was able to garner international attention by baiting Bull Connor into abusing the protesters.
    D. was able to convince President Kennedy to come to Birmingham to inspect the conditions.

7.	James Baldwin saw Martin Luther King as trapped by the conflicting expectations of Whites and Blacks. He viewed the Civil Rights Movement as an opportunity to
    A. re-conceptualize an African American identity independent of white America.
    B. unify the African American community and finally have one accepted leader.
    C. build a strong religious tradition that accepted the Christian ethos.
    D. build a generation of fighters who would defend Black America.

8.   In James Baldwin's provocative book <u>The Fire Next Time</u>, Baldwin warned
      A. Blacks needed to be integrated immediately into mainstream America.
      B. African American youth were not going to accept anything but violent solutions.
      C. Blacks and Whites had to accept their multiracial culture or they would destroy each other.
      D. if the world didn't accept Dr. King's message, then someone more violent would come.

9.   Robert Moses wanted to challenge the Mississippi political order by registering African Americans to vote. To gain national attention he instituted a controversial strategy called the Mississippi Summer Project. What did this project do?
      A. It organized Black Mississippi voters into Republican Leaguers who backed candidates.
      B. He brought middle and upper class White students to Mississippi to register Blacks to vote.
      C. He formed a new organization made up of White women and Black men to encourage racial understanding.
      D. He found Black candidates who were willing to run for office in Mississippi.

10.   One of the most significant accomplishments of the Summer Project was the creation of the Mississippi Freedom Democratic Party. Who was the person who galvanized national attention to African American conditions in Mississippi?
      A. James Farmer
      B. Robert Moses
      C. Fannie Lou Hamer
      D. Stokely Carmichael

11.   Malcolm X was one of the most inspirational African American leaders of the early 1960s. All of the following are true of Malcolm X, <u>EXCEPT</u> he
      A. was the national spokesperson for the Nation of Islam.
      B. was responsible for bringing Muhammad Ali into the Nation of Islam.
      C. had a religious transformation after making a Hajji to Mecca.
      D. was more interested in national issues than he was in international issues.

12.   The 1965 Selma to Montgomery March proved to be a defining moment in the Civil Rights struggle. Which of the following best describes what inspired the march and what it accomplished?
      A. Martin Luther's call for immediate integration of the schools. The schools in Selma, Alabama were integrated.
      B. The effort to recall Governor George Wallace. The state had a new election which Wallace won.
      C. Jimmy Lee Jackson was murdered during a voting rights demonstration. President Johnson signed the Voting Rights Act.
      D. Rev. Fred Shuttlesworth's house was bombed. The FBI arrested two Klansmen for the bombing.

13. The Black Panther Party was organized in Lowndes County, Alabama after the Selma to Montgomery March to encourage African Americans to take control of their political institutions. Who founded this organization?
    A. John L. Lewis
    B. H. Rap Brown
    C. Stokely Carmichael
    D. Robert Moses

14. As SNCC leaders increasingly moved from an emphasis on integration to an emphasis on Black Power, they
    A. purged the organization of White members and became more radical.
    B. increasingly worked with Dr. King and his movement.
    C. demanded that the NAACP leaders also join SNCC and advocate Black Power.
    D. increased their membership of radical White youths who espoused violence.

15. Just before his death Malcolm X had organized a new organization dedicated to human rights. Which organization did he found?
    A. The Negro Progressive Conference
    B. The Organization of African American Unity
    C. The Black Islamic Brotherhood
    D. The Brotherhood of the Fruit of Islam

THOUGHT QUESTIONS

1. Discuss the strengths and weaknesses of the Kennedy administration as they dealt with civil rights.

2. Using the account of Fannie Lou Hamer, what were some of the consequences of participating in civil rights activities?

3. Describe the internal struggles between the various civil rights organizations. How did these battles hamper their success in several protests?

4. Why was the March on Washington seen as such a watershed event in American History? How does it represent a new strategy for expressing discontent?

5. Describe the role that White students played in dramatizing the necessity for new civil rights laws.

6. Discuss the role that Malcolm X played during the late 1950s and early 1960s. How should he be viewed in terms of the Civil Rights Movement?

7. How did the shift from civil rights to Black Power transform the goals and actions of those struggling for civil rights? Did this shift help or hurt the movement?

ANSWER KEY MULTIPLE CHOICE QUESTIONS

1. B
2. D
3. D
4. B
5. D
6. D
7. A
8. C
9. B
10. C
11. D
12. C
13. C
14. A
15. B

CHAPTER 19 *Resistance, Repression, and Retrenchment: 1967–1978*

CHAPTER SUMMARY

Opening Vignette: Hubert "Rap" Brown Proclaims Black Power

Standing on a car trunk in Cambridge, Maryland, in July 1967, newly elected SNCC chair "Rap" Brown proclaimed, "Violence is as American as apple pie." An advocate of armed self-defense, Brown sounded themes of racial pride and militancy. Though he was not responsible, Cambridge erupted in violence the next day—one of many rebellions in the "long, hot summer" of 1967 and "dress rehearsal," said Brown, "for real revolution."

A New Racial Consciousness

In the same political climate that produced Brown's calls for revolution, Marxist Angela Davis blamed capitalism for American racism. Escalating protests against the war in Vietnam and the military draft also challenged authority and heightened militancy. But the new black consciousness was at least as much a cultural phenomenon as it was political activism. Black students began to adopt natural "afro" hairstyles and wear African-style clothing. Proponents of black cultural nationalism called for African or African American values. In time, this black cultural transformation would be just as influential as the era's political militancy.

King and the Wars against Communism and Poverty

Black power controversies and the upsurge in racial violence posed a dilemma for Martin Luther King, who saw that the African American freedom struggle had not transformed legal rights into better living conditions. Though reluctant to enter the national debate over Vietnam, he changed his mind on seeing images of burned and wounded children. In April 1967, at Riverside Church in New York, he publicly criticized the war. Challenging those who said he should stick to racial issues, he charged that the war consumed funds that might otherwise be used to fight poverty in black communities and also noted that black war casualties were disproportionately high. He could not speak out, he said, against "the violence in the oppressed ghettos without having first spoke clearly to the greatest purveyor of violence in the world today: my own government." King remained committed to nonviolence despite Black Power challenges, the black nationalism of Amiri Baraka, the failures of SCLC's Operation Breadbasket in Chicago, and insurgencies in northern cities. Yet he was targeted by the FBI. Johnson was angered by King's antiwar stance. Split over Vietnam and divided by deteriorating relations between blacks and Jews, the old civil rights coalition, and the Democratic Party, weakened.

Determined to reverse the cycle of escalating racial violence and declining white support for racial reform, King initiated a Poor People's Campaign. In Memphis to support a black sanitation workers' strike, he was assassinated. His death prompted outbursts of racial violence in more than one hundred communities. But even the shared outpouring of grief could not bridge the deep political divisions hampering his work in his final years.

81

Black Soldiers in Vietnam

For Army Major Colin Powell, King's death was an "abrupt reminder" that "racism still bedeviled America." But he and other black officers in Vietnam rejected Black Power militancy. "We were not eager to see the country burned down. We were doing well in it." As in previous wars, Vietnam offered black solders a chance to demonstrate that they were prepared to fight for their nation. But the backdrop of violence on the home front and the battlefields shaped the way racial issues were viewed and discussed. And young black draftees, serving disproportionately in combat roles, increasingly resented those in authority, including Powell and other officers. Finishing his tour in Vietnam, Powell was disillusioned with the conduct of the war. Although it marked the culmination of the desegregation of the armed forces, it also indicated that the military was not isolated from the racial problems that affected American society.

The Rise and Fall of Black Power Militancy

Meanwhile, the Black Panther Party was urging black men not to "fight and kill other people of color in the world," who were also "victimized by the white racist government of America." Founded by Bobby Seale and Huey Newton in Oakland, California, the party drafted a ten-point platform with far-reaching demands. Most notable was its call for an end to police brutality against black people. Panther Eldridge Cleaver's best-selling *Soul on Ice* expressed a new black militancy based on a bold black heterosexual masculinity. Seale and Cleaver recruited Stokely Carmichael, aiming to ally with SNCC. The Panthers expanded rapidly as dozens of chapters were organized across the nation.

The growth of the Panthers coincided with the expansion of black studies programs at American universities and increased admission of black students. Collective protests by black athletes culminating at an awards ceremony at the 1968 Olympic games at which gold metal winners raised their fists in the Black Power salute. Panther influence sparked a growing activism among prison inmates, supported by Davis, who was implicated in courthouse shootings, and evidenced by an uprising at Attica, in New York, which was violently suppressed. Although the tactics of storming Attica were criticized, there was also increasing support among white Americans for law-and-order politics.

Meanwhile, the FBI and its counterintelligence unit, COINTELPRO, designed to disrupt black nationalists groups, targeted the Panthers with infiltration and "dirty tricks." Even as they depicted themselves as spearheading black revolution, the party was beset with legal problems and internal divisions over leadership and ideology. By the early 1970s, Black Power militancy was no longer a significant political force. But Hollywood turned this new assertiveness into popular entertainment with "blaxploitation" films, featuring violence-prone black male heroes.

Diverging Directions of Black Politics

As Jesse Jackson, a King protégé, transformed Operation Breadbasket into People United to Serve Humanity (PUSH), he also transformed militancy into a practical political style. Electoral politics was supplanting black radicalism, and Jackson best expressed the mood of the 1972 National Black Political Convention in Gary, Indiana. In attendance were black mayors,

Congressional Black Caucus members, union representatives, and the Black Arts Movement leader Baraka. Though some black militants were present, the gathering was dominated by those who had moved away from black power radicalism. The unity achieved at Gary was short-lived, especially after ties with the Democratic Party were reaffirmed and Shirley Chisholm, running for president, was ignored by black delegates. But as the number of black elected officials grew, they proved increasingly able to guide African American politics at the national level.

As black nationalist political militancy receded, black nationalism emphasized the cultural and psychological transformation of African Americans. The cultural and intellectual aspects of the Black Power movement were institutionalized in black community organizations and African American academic programs. An inward focus was evident in an outpouring of poetry by black women. Alex Haley's *Roots*, a fictionalized account of his family's history, promoted both African American history and sparked genealogical research among both blacks and whites. Its popularity as a television series made it a source of education, as well as entertainment.

Although Thurgood Marshall was named to the Supreme Court, he was increasingly out of step with the court's conservative direction. Rulings set limits on busing as a means of school integration and overturned affirmative action policies that set aside a number of places for black students. In Congress, Barbara Jordan's articulate analysis of the Watergate scandal's constitutional issues brought her national attention and an invitation to be the keynote speaker at the 1976 Democratic National Convention. Jimmy Carter's election to the presidency that year exemplified the new racial politics, for he had campaigned as pro–civil rights southerner able to attract black support without alienating white Democrats. Carter appointed prominent African Americans to high positions in his administration, notably Andrew Young as ambassador to the United Nations, Eleanor Holmes Norton as chair of the Equal Employment Opportunity Commission, and former SNCC chair John Lewis as associate director of Action, the federal volunteer agency. Nationwide, hundreds of black candidates were winning office, among the many unmistakable signs of black progress was increasing racial tolerance.

LEARNING OBJECTIVES

Students should be able to

- describe the new role of African Americans in film.
- discuss the emergence of the Black Arts movement.
- examine the political ideas of new African-American organizations.
- describe the legal strides and setbacks for African Americans.
- explain how some black political groups became more militant during this period.

IDENTIFICATIONS

Explain the significance of each of the following:

1. Hubert "Rap" Brown

2. Angela Yvonne Davis

3. Muhammad Ali

4. Sydney Poitier

5. Martin Luther King, Jr.

6. Jesse Jackson

7. Stokely Carmichael

8. Amiri Baraka

9. COINTELPRO

10. Poor People's Campaign

11. James Earl Ray

12. Colin Powell

13. Vietnam War

14. Black Panther Party for Self Defense

15. Bobby Seal

16. Huey Newton

17. Eldridge Cleaver

18. Black Studies

19. Harry Edwards

20. Tommie Smith

21. John Carlos

22. Maulana Karenga

23. George Jackson

24. Attica

25. Mario Van Peebles

26. Blaxploitation Films

27. PUSH

28. Shirley Chisholm

29. Thurgood Marshall

30. Bakke decision

31. Barbara Jordan

32. Jimmy Carter

33. Cicely Tyson

34. Roots

35. Alex Haley

MULTIPLE CHOICE

1.   Angela Davis's radicalism was inspired by all of the following forces <u>EXCEPT</u>
        A. her parent's activity in civil rights causes.
        B. her years in a private school in New York.
        C. the discrimination her family faced in Birmingham, Alabama.
        D. the harassment she endured during her 10-year marriage to a White man.

2.   Dr. Martin Luther King, Jr.'s decision to publicly condemn the Vietnam war was inspired by all of the following <u>EXCEPT</u>
        A. his desire to end the struggle between him and the new SNCC leaders.
        B. an article he read in *Ramparts* magazine showing disturbing pictures of victims of American bombing.
        C. his growing realization that the war was immoral and draining needed resources.
        D. his desire to show critics that he was not a stooge of the Johnson administration.

3.	According to Dr. Martin Luther King, Jr., the most vicious and frightful protestors that he faced were those in
	A.	Jackson, Mississippi.
	B.	Birmingham, Alabama.
	C.	Chicago, Illinois.
	D.	St. Augustine, Florida.

4.	Muhammad Ali captured the world's attention and sympathy when he took on the Federal government to defend his religious beliefs. What did Ali do?
	A.	He refused to fight Black Muslim boxers in segregated arenas.
	B.	He refused induction into the U.S. Army to fight in Vietnam.
	C.	He refused to denounce the Nation of Islam and its policy of self-defense.
	D.	He participated in several anti-government rallies calling for integration.

5.	Dr. Martin Luther King, Jr. was outmaneuvered and defeated in his Chicago campaign by Chicago's politically savvy mayor. Who was he?
	A.	Laurie Pritchett
	B.	Bull Connor
	C.	Richard Daley
	D.	Stanley Simpson

6.	In 1967 the nation experienced serious racial upheavals in both Detroit and Newark. These violent outbursts were influenced by all of the following EXCEPT
	A.	the growing popularity of books advocating violence like Wretched of the Earth.
	B.	the growing influence of Black Power advocates who supported violence as an alternative.
	C.	the constant hopelessness and frustration of the residents.
	D.	the lack of African American police officers on the city's payroll.

7.	By 1967 Dr. Martin Luther King, Jr. shifted the struggle for rights from a fight for civil rights to a struggle for
	A.	economic justice and the problems of the poor.
	B.	anti-war activities and student organizations protesting war.
	C.	the struggle of migrant workers in the west and southwest.
	D.	the South African struggle to end apartheid.

8.	Dr. Martin Luther King, Jr. went to Memphis, Tennessee in 1968 to
	A.	help recruit people to his Poor People's Campaign.
	B.	to aid striking African American sanitation workers.
	C.	to organize a protest against stores that continued to segregate.
	D.	to support an African American candidate running for office in the city.

9. Colin Powell summed up the frustrations of African American soldiers in Vietnam when he said:
   A. Black GIs if lucky get home still to face poor job prospects and fresh indignities.
   B. The Vietnamese are not the enemy of Black southerners.
   C. America has not done a good job of training Black soldiers.
   D. The U.S. Army does not provide Black soldiers advancement opportunities.

10. Eldridge Cleaver played a pivotal role in expanding the role and direction of the Black Panther Party when he
    A. raped White women to demonstrate his frustration with the American system.
    B. recruited Stokely Carmichael and his international allies in the struggle to free Huey Newton.
    C. wrote his book Soul on Ice, a collection of essays about urban life.
    D. ran for president as the Peace and Freedom party candidate.

11. During the late 1960s African American college students suddenly became active again. They protested all of the following EXCEPT
    A. the lack of Black Studies Programs at the schools.
    B. the expansion of the Vietnam War.
    C. racism associated with the Olympic games.
    D. the lack of Black officers in the United States military.

12. The United States government was obsessed with preventing a Black messiah from rising within the Black community. To prevent this, the FBI did all of the following EXCEPT
    A. open several COINTELPRO operations against the major Black figures.
    B. undermine the strength and success of several Black organizations by infiltrating them with spies.
    C. participate in deadly raids which killed and arrested leading Black figures.
    D. pay huge bribes to entice leaders to keep quiet.

13. African American political leaders expanded their scope and moved into national politics during the 1970s. All of the following are examples of African Americans developing a national agenda EXCEPT
    A. the National Black Political Convention.
    B. People United to Serve Humanity.
    C. Shirley Chisholm's run for the presidency.
    D. the Black Political Agenda.
    E. all of the above.

14. The Bakke case was a watershed event for African Americans because it
    A. threatened the future of the highly successful program called affirmative action.
    B. transformed California into a Republican state.
    C. said that race could never be used as a factor when awarding contracts.
    D. virtually reversed the Brown v. Board of Education decision.

15. Movies like the television series *Roots* and commercial films transformed the movie industry for African American film makers in all of these ways <u>EXCEPT</u>
    A. they provided positive roles for African American women.
    B. fostered an appreciation for African American history while drawing attention to America's brutal past.
    C. provided an opportunity for talented African American artist and actors to show their talents.
    D. created a huge revenue stream for Black directors who wanted to produce films.

THOUGHT QUESTIONS

1. Discuss how the Vietnam War worked to splinter the many factions of the civil rights coalition.

2. How did the shift from nonviolence to violence mark a shift in the civil rights movement and work to undermine the efforts of Martin Luther King, Jr.?

3. Discuss why African American soldiers were so morally conflicted during the Vietnam War.

4. Describe how the Black Panther Platform can be viewed as a progressive document calling for a just society.

5. Discuss why Pauli Murray viewed the call for Black Power as so destructive.

6. Describe the goals of African American activist after 1968. How did the government and society react to their demands?

7. What were the gains of African American politicians during the 1970s? Why did the nation seem to retreat from its commitment to civil rights?

8. Discuss how the increase in African American films that told stories of African American triumph changed the Hollywood film industry.

ANSWER KEY MULTIPLE CHOICE QUESTIONS

1. D
2. D
3. C
4. B
5. C
6. D
7. A
8. B
9. A
10. B
11. D
12. D
13. E
14. A
15. D

CHAPTER 20 *The Search for New Directions During a Conservative Era, 1979–1991*

CHAPTER SUMMARY

Opening Vignette: Michele Wallace on the Discontents of Black Women

Michele Wallace had sympathized with the civil rights movement and admired Black Power advocates. But in the late 1960s she was transformed by the emerging women's movement. In *Black Macho* (1979), she challenged the black militancy that equated black liberation with a violent assertion of black manhood, exposing tensions between black men and women and other conflicts among African Americans in a conservative era.

Finding a Place in the Political System

After Andrew Young, U.S. ambassador to the United Nations, met informally with a representative of the Palestine Liberation Organization, objections by Jewish-American leaders forced his resignation. The episode bred black distrust of the Democratic Party, as President Jimmy Carter seemed willing to forgo black support for Jewish support. Black leaders had more to fear, though, from incoming president Ronald Reagan, a conservative who exploited anti-tax sentiment and white resentment of black "welfare mothers."

A Black Alternatives Conference in 1980 revealed disillusionment with governmental programs like affirmative action, and heralded a new black conservatism. Some black conservatives advocated self-help in the tradition of Booker T. Washington and Marcus Garvey. Others, like libertarian economist Thomas Sowell, claimed that government action to combat discrimination was counterproductive, producing a debilitating "culture of poverty" passed down through generations, creating what sociologist William Julius Wilson called an "underclass," falling behind the rest of society. Though Wilson argued that the black middle class had benefited from civil rights reforms and affirmative action, Sowell's influence marked the beginning of a broad shift away from the liberal assumptions underlying the social policies of Franklin Roosevelt and Lyndon Johnson.

Reagan, elected with little black support, indicated that his administration would be less responsive than Carter's to civil rights concerns. He reduced funding for welfare and other programs that supported the poor, with the result that black unemployment and the number of African American families below the poverty line grew. After he appointed Clarence Thomas, a critic of busing and affirmative action, to head the Equal Employment Opportunity Commission, the agency's budget and staff declined. But in Reagan's second term, Martin Luther King's birthday was made a national holiday.

Jesse Jackson's 1984 Presidential Campaign

Jesse Jackson's forceful criticisms of Reagan contributed to his emergence as the nation's most influential black political figure. Building on the anger over Young's forced resignation, Jackson traveled to the Middle East, meeting with PLO leader Arafat, thus further offending Jewish leaders. He returned to support Harold Washington's successful campaign for mayor of Chicago by emphasizing voter registration, and in 1984 he decided to run for president, figuring that if African Americans could gain the balance of power within the Democratic Party they could force it to support progressive politics. Jackson expressed strong support for civil rights, labor unions, women's rights, and environmental causes. His campaign received a boost when his negotiations secured the release of a black Navy pilot shot down over Syria following the failure of the State Department to do so. But his early successes collapsed following an anti-Semitic remark magnified in comments by Nation of Islam leader Louis Farrakhan. Though Walter Mondale got the party nomination and Reagan won the election, Jackson, with his "rainbow coalition" appeal, demonstrated that a black candidate could draw white support.

In Washington, Eleanor Holmes Norton, Mary Frances Berry, and Walter Fauntroy founded the Free South Africa Movement, and repeated protests at the embassy strengthened the campaign to force South Africa to end apartheid. Campus activists compelled universities such as Stanford and Columbia to divest endowment funds from companies that did business in South Africa. Ultimately, Congress overrode Reagan's veto to institute economic sanctions against South Africa, the first time since the 1960s that African Americans had spearheaded a national campaign of nonviolent direct action.

The Popularization of Black Feminism

Alice Walker, a participant in the Free South Africa movement and a qualified defender of *Black Macho*, attracted controversy with her best-selling novel *The Color Purple*. Like Zora Neale Hurston, Walker focused on relationships within black families rather than on external black-white relations, revealing the brutality of gender oppression and the indomitable spirit of a woman who endures and ultimately prevails. The book's film version made stars of Whoopi Goldberg, Oprah Winfrey, and Danny Glover, but director Steven Spielberg was criticized for turning male characters into caricatures.

Walker's success built on a foundation established by earlier black women writers, including Hurston. Maya Angelou's autobiographical *I Know Why the Caged Bird Sings* was widely studied as a metaphor for women's oppression. The fiction of Toni Morrison and Gloria Naylor, together with the works of influential black women poets, blended militant feminist advocacy and intimate revelation of black women's perspectives on male-female relations. Their criticisms of black males made them vulnerable to charges of racial disloyalty, and all faced a dilemma as they sought to depict African American life accurately but also positively.

TV dramas featuring black families were primarily sit-coms, and Hollywood produced formulaic black characters who lacked ties to realistic black communities. Following *The Color Purple*, however, black actors increasingly moved into primary or co-starring roles. Although hit movies of the 1980s, such as *Trading Places,* used predictable racial culture clash themes, a few films, such as *A Soldier's Story* and *Glory,* made serious attempts to illuminate African American life

92

and history. Director Spike Lee demonstrated the possibilities for significant African American films outside the studio system, while August Wilson's plays were praised for their sensitive portrayal of African American family relationships.

Meanwhile, the popularity of hip hop and gangsta rap indicated a competing black cultural trend with lyrics that sometimes degraded women and celebrated an outlaw lifestyle of sex, drugs, and violence. But rap was also controversial, and a large segment became highly politicized, the most overt social agenda in popular music since the urban folk movement of the 1960s.

Racial Progress and Internal Tensions

Jesse Jackson's second presidential campaign, in 1988, garnered greater support than his first, but it also exposed growing divisions among African Americans. Many Democratic leaders saw him as a liability, believing the party needed to distance itself from the causes he championed. Republican George Bush won the election, in part by inciting white racial prejudice in TV attack ads. The Democrats' defeat reinforced the party's tendency to veer away from its tradition of civil rights reform.

Despite black conservatives' arguments that affirmative action and other racial preference programs were no longer necessary, the nation continued to be beset by racial problems—all unaddressed by the Reagan and Bush administrations. Colin Powell's appointment as head of the Joint Chiefs of Staff indicated that individual African Americans could excel, but when Bush nominated Thomas to replace Thurgood Marshall on the Supreme Court, a new controversy erupted. Already opposed by civil rights and feminist groups, Thomas was accused by Anita Hill, an EEOC lawyer when he headed the agency, of sexual harassment. Her testimony set off a contentious national debate on issues of class, gender, race, and ideology that marked the convergence of the past decade's cultural and political trends. By a slim margin, Thomas's nomination was confirmed, but Norton credited Hill for the upsurge in political activity among women that helped make 1992 "The Year of the Woman," in which a record number of women were elected to national office.

LEARNING OBJECTIVES

Students should be able to

- discuss the conservative views of many African Americans.
- explain the connection between the American civil rights and the South African anti-apartheid Movements.
- describe the arguments made by feminist black women regarding gender roles in the black community.
- discuss the different ways that American media portrayed African Americans at the same time that blacks began to shape American media.

IDENTIFICATIONS

Explain the significance of each of the following:

1. Michele Wallace

2. Andrew Young

3. Clarence Thomas

4. Thomas Sowell

5. William Julius Wilson

6. Mary Frances Berry

7. Coretta Scott King

8. Jesse Jackson

9. Operation PUSH

10. Harold Washington

11. Louis Farrakhan

12. Nelson Mandela

13. Desmond Tutu

14. Alice Walker

15. Toni Morrison

16. Bill Cosby

17. Eddie Murphy

18. Denzel Washington

19. Spike Lee

20. August Wilson

21. Last Poets

22. Public Enemy

23. NWA

24. George Bush

25. Lawrence Douglass Wilder

26. Colin Powell

27. Anita Hill

28. Clarence Thomas

MULTIPLE CHOICE QUESTIONS

1.   Anita Hill accused Supreme Court nominee Clarence Thomas of sexual harassment when they worked at which of the following?
        A. The Justice Department in the Carter administration
        B. The Solicitor General's office in the first Bush administration
        C. The EEOC Office of the Reagan administration
        D. The Agriculture Department in the Ford administration

2.   Jesse Jackson's first run for the presidency was largely undermined by his association with
        A. Eldridge Cleaver and the Black Panther Party
        B. Angela Davis and Communism
        C. Louis Farrakhan and the Nation of Islam
        D. Andrew Young and Anti-Semitism

3.   The Hip Hop craze of the 1980s can be traced back to all of the following EXCEPT
        A. The Last Poets.
        B. 1970s Funk musicians.
        C. street poets.
        D. Negro Spirituals.

4.   Alice Walker was vehemently criticized for her portrayal of African Americans in her book *The Color Purple*. All of the following were Black complaints EXCEPT
        A. it aired the dirty laundry of African Americans.
        B. there were no positive roles for African American men.
        C. the book did not cover a contemporary issue.
        D. the book gave White Americans too much power over African American lives.

5. In order for African American entertainers to have success, they had to navigate the racial landscape. Who was the most successful African American film star of the 1980s?
    A. Bill Cosby
    B. Denzel Washington
    C. Morgan Freeman
    D. Eddie Murphy

6. In 1986 African Americans joined forces with others to get which of the following passed over President Reagan's objections?
    A. The Martin Luther King Holiday
    B. The Comprehensive Anti-Apartheid Act
    C. The 1986 Civil Rights Act
    D. The African Debt Relief Act

7. African Americans pulled off one of the most important political victories in Chicago when they elected an African American mayor. Who was he?
    A. Harold Washington
    B. Coleman Young
    C. Carl Stokes
    D. Thomas Bradley

8. Thomas Sowell is best known
    A. for his defense of affirmative action.
    B. for his opposition to Reaganomics.
    C. as a Black conservative.
    D. for his strong support of military expansion.

9. Rap music became a controversial musical genre during the 1980s. To curb the spread and influence of this music, politicians suggested
    A. outlawing Rap music.
    B. placing warning labels on the music.
    C. censorship of the music.
    D. fining rap musicians for inappropriate lyrics.

10. During the 1980s movies attempted to illuminate African American life and history. All of the following are examples EXCEPT
    A. *A Soldier's Story.*
    B. *Glory.*
    C. *She's Got To Have It.*
    D. *Shaft in Africa.*

11. Alice Walker's *Color Purple* dramatizes the heroic struggle of African American women against
    A. White racism.
    B. Black male chauvinism.
    C. poverty and segregation.
    D. female role expectations.

12. During the 1970s and the 1980s there was a dramatic increase in interest of readers in authentic African American voices. All of the following were women who gained prominence during this period <u>EXCEPT</u>
    A. Maya Angelou.
    B. Toni Morrison.
    C. Gloria Naylor.
    D. Zora Neale Hurston.

13. As part of the Free South Africa Campaign, who did African Americans want to free from prison?
    A. Nelson Mandela
    B. Desmond Tutu
    C. Steve Biko
    D. Maulana Karenga

14. Jesse Jackson received international acclaim in January 1984 when he
    A. started a new organization called Rainbow Push.
    B. defeated Ronald Reagan in the Democratic Primary in South Carolina.
    C. flew to Syria and won the release of Robert O. Goodman, an American pilot.
    D. conducted an international conference on the Arab-Israeli crisis.

15. Conservatives believed that welfare programs and programs such as affirmative action created a governmental dependency which was not healthy. Therefore they called for all of the following <u>EXCEPT</u>
    A. stiffer penalties to punish those with criminal behavior.
    B. forcing welfare recipients to work or get off welfare.
    C. cuts in government-funded anti-poverty programs.
    D. decreasing spending on public education.

THOUGHT QUESTIONS

1. Explain how Jesse Jackson's speech to the 1984 Democratic convention was designed to appeal those who opposed the Reagan Revolution.

2. Discuss the beliefs of Thomas Sowell and other Black conservatives regarding race-specific programs.

3. How does the declaration in *A Radical Black Feminist Statement* seem to set an angry tone by African American women? What are the issues that seem to bother them?

4. Describe the significance of the Free South Africa movement for improving race relations in the U.S.

5. Describe how African American women demonstrated a more liberated attitude in their writing during the 1970s and 80s.

6. What were the cultural conflicts played out in the entertainment industry during the 1980s? For example, what types of conflicts existed in *The Cosby Show* and Gangster rap?

7. Explain how the debate between Clarence Thomas and Anita Hill highlights one divide within the African American community.

ANSWER KEY MULTIPLE CHOICE QUESTIONS

1. C
2. C
3. D
4. D
5. D
6. B
7. A
8. C
9. C
10. D
11. B
12. D
13. A
14. C
15. D

CHAPTER 21, *Continuing Struggles Over Rights and Identity, 1992–Present*

CHAPTER SUMMARY

Opening Vignette: Oprah Winfrey and Social Healing

In 1992, Oprah Winfrey took her popular talk show to Los Angeles, so viewers could see the violence following the verdict in the Rodney King beating case. The riot was an indicator that serious racial and economic problems remained unsolved. Oprah's interviews, which encouraged residents and viewers to understand the perspectives of others, revealed the diversity of African American lives and opportunities following the civil rights movement and the rise of black feminism.

A New Day for African Americans?

The poem Maya Angelou presented at Bill Clinton's presidential inauguration in 1993 was both patriotic and provocative, referring to the "wretched pain" of American history for those who "arrived on a nightmare praying for a dream." Clinton's invitation to a black poet reflected his desire to reach out to African Americans. Like Jimmy Carter, his victory was due to the overwhelming support of black voters, and he responded by appointing an unprecedented number of African Americans to high posts. But like other Democratic presidents, Clinton was reluctant to take controversial stands on racial issues. When Lani Guinier, his nominee for head of the Justice Department's Civil Rights Division, was attacked by conservatives for her views on political representation, Clinton failed to defend her. She saw Clinton's capitulation as "an unfortunate metaphor" for the way black people continued to be defined, and misrepresented, by other people.

While the civil rights movement seemed to be part of history, civil rights issues had not gone away, as the King beating and controversies over affirmative action indicated. Cornel West's *Race Matters* (1993) pointed to the widespread mistreatment of black men by law enforcement agencies. Marion Wright Edelman pointed to the widespread poverty of African Americans that disadvantaged black children. The issue of welfare reform revived old debates about whether black poverty derived from enduring racial inequalities or from deficiencies in the values and attitudes of poor people. Clinton's comprehensive welfare reform put many on welfare into the expanding workforce, and poverty rates for African Americans fell from 33 percent in 1993 to 24 percent in 2000. But even for the working poor, poverty was a reality.

Race and the Criminal Justice System

Rodney King inadvertently became a symbol of the troubled relationship between inner-city African Americans and predominantly white police forces. The issue of police prejudice and brutality rose again to the forefront when popular football star O. J. Simpson was tried for murder. Johnny Cochran, Simpson's lawyer, transformed the proceedings from a murder case involving a black celebrity into a public indictment of racism in law enforcement. Knowing from experience that the Los Angeles police could not be relied on to conduct an unbiased investigation involving a black man, Cochran planted seeds of doubt in the minds of jurors, who acquitted Simpson. Polls revealed that most African Americans agreed with the verdict, while most white Americans did not. Clearly the legal proceedings left larger questions unanswered—about different racial reactions, the sympathies of the predominantly female jury, and the centrality of money and class, as a black millionaire had been set free by the efforts of a highly paid defense team.

The Prison System of Racial Control

Angela Davis, herself imprisoned during the 1970s, led a campaign against what she termed "the prison industrial complex," claiming that Americans used "mass incarceration" as a solution for unemployment and a substitute for social justice. The total prison population topped two million, disproportionately large compared to other nations and disproportionately African American: about 12 percent of black males in their twenties were in jail. The consequences—for individuals, families, and voting rights—were significant. The persistence of black poverty and explosion of drug use contributed to the increase in the prison population, as did law-and-order politicians who strengthened the hand of the police. Following civil rights reforms, police bias was subtle rather than overt, indicated by slow response times for black neighborhoods and longer sentences for black criminals. Racial profiling by police and increased surveillance increased the probability that African Americans would be arrested. Even affluent black male motorists were subject to police checks for what was termed "driving while black."

Following the assassination of Malcolm X, Louis Farrakhan was the somewhat unlikely inheritor of his legacy. Farrakhan reestablished the remnant of the Nation of Islam under his leadership, and his controversial statements reflected the anger and frustration of many disaffected African Americans. In October 1995, he provided inspiration for the Million Man March, the largest gathering of African Americans in the nation's history. Revealing the widespread concern among African Americans about the problems affecting black families, organizers promoted the march as an opportunity for black men to atone for past misdeeds and to commit themselves to take responsibility for their families and communities. Jesse Jackson, the primary black leader of the previous decade, was reduced to delivering a preliminary speech for Farrakhan.

Rethinking the Meaning of Race

In 1997 President Clinton called on eminent black historian John Hope Franklin to lead a national "conversation about race." The challenge was enormous, given the racial controversies that burst into public view during the 1990s. The large question was the significance of race in American life. Shelby Steele and other black conservatives complained of the deleterious effects of a "victim-focused black identity," while West and others insisted that racial prejudices and discrimination still shaped the lives and identities of African Americans. Franklin's panel concluded that the most pressing racial problems no longer involved overt acts of violence but were indicated in subtle practices that kept African Americans in subordinate economic positions despite civil rights laws.

Among the challenges Franklin's panel faced was how to deal with the contemporary consequences of past racial injustices. Legal challenges continued to narrow affirmative action programs in university admissions even as proponents argued that diversity itself was of value. Reparations as a means for compensating African Americans for slavery and discrimination made little headway, but a few local settlement cases were successful, and all Americans were increasingly aware of historical injustices.

Marlon Riggs's films contributed to the national dialogue on race, especially for promoting a unity based on "talking to each other" and understanding the diversity and complexity of African American lives. His work reflected a trend in African American thought toward recognizing that racial identity was not permanent but constantly changing. Though being black was an identity forced on all Americans with African ancestry, it was also chosen by all who came to see themselves as a group not only oppressed but struggling against oppression.

Another theme of popular culture highlighted individuals crossing cultural boundaries. As white Americans became more African American in cultural outlook and African Americans became more like other Americans, African American identity became more complex. When the 2000 census allowed people, for the first time, to choose more than one category to identify their ancestry, more than 7 million Americans did so. As the meaning of race continued to be debated, African American historical memory became more essential. Rather than being rooted in African ancestry or in the shared experience of oppression and resistance, African American identity came to be increasingly rooted in understanding African history.

Democracy and the Legacy of Race

Martin Luther King II charged that the presidential election of 2000 was a distortion of democracy, pointing to the removal of more than 94,000 Florida residents from the voter registration roles. King's complaint about the erroneous disqualification of voters was only one way the contested election highlighted the continuing relationship between African American history and American democracy. The Electoral College system, which advantages sparsely settled states, was another, as the election raised Guinier's concern that an electoral system should accurately reflect the votes of all adult citizens.

Though George W. Bush became president with minimal black support, he appointed African Americans to high posts, including Colin Powell as secretary of state and Condoleezza Rise as national security adviser. Their prominence was atypical, however, and in the war on terrorism that followed the attacks of September 11, 2001, and especially in the invasion of Iraq, African American critics of America's foreign policy reflected their distinctive experiences and awareness of the struggles and sacrifices required to achieve freedom and democracy at home, much less abroad.

LEARNING OBJECTIVES

Students should be able to

- describe the diversity of African American thought following the civil rights movement.
- discuss the challenges still facing African Americans.
- examine the effects of poverty on black Americans.
- explain the differing viewpoints regarding black identity.

IDENTIFICATIONS

Explain the significance of each of the following:

1. Oprah Winfrey

2. Maya Angelou

3. Bill Clinton

4. Cornel West

5. Lani Guinier

6. Marion Wright Edelman

7. Rodney King

8. O.J. Simpson

9. Johnnie Cochran

10. Angela Davis

11. Louis Farrakhan

12. Nation of Islam

13. Million Man March

14. John Hope Franklin

15. Abner Louima

16. James Byrd Jr.

17. Affirmative Action

18. Marlon Riggs

19. Condoleeza Rice

20. Colin Powell

MULTIPLE CHOICE

1.	The 2000 Census showed that the nation was becoming a much more racially diverse area. However, the challenge for African Americans is that
    A. the White population continues to grow at a faster rate.
    B. the Hispanic population is identifying more and more with Whites.
    C. the African American population is the oldest group in the country.
    D. increasing numbers of Americans are choosing to define themselves as *multiethnic.*

2.	The cases of James Byrd and Abner Louima were proof that
    A. crimes against Blacks would be punished.
    B. racist violence was not dead in America.
    C. Black on Black crimes was being reduced.
    D. America had solved its race problem.

3.	The verdict in the Simpson case seems to suggest that
    A. White people were willing to excuse the crimes of a popular African American athlete.
    B. African Americans were willing to convict Blacks accused of crimes.
    C. Wealth seemed to trump race when it came to criminal trials.
    D. African Americans and Whites seemed to see justice the same way.

4.	All <u>BUT</u> which one of the following were the actions of President Clinton that caused Toni Morrison to refer to him as the nation's first Black president?
    A. He appointed more African Americans to top positions than any other president.
    B. He was very comfortable in predominantly African American settings.
    C. He was a strong supporter of racial quotas.
    D. He chose an African American poet to read at his inauguration.

5.	Lani Guinier argued that under the present system minorities' rights were often ignored by the majority. How did conservatives attack these views and wreck her nomination to head the Civil Rights division of the Justice Department?
    A. They called her a quota queen.
    B. They said that she was a racist.
    C. They accused her of wanting an all-Black Congress.
    D. They supported her and her ideas.

6. The rising number of African American youth incarcerated in prison hurts the African American community in all of the following ways EXCEPT
    A. it reduces the number of eligible men for young women to marry.
    B. it reduces the number of African Americans who can participate in the political process.
    C. it adds to the popular notion that African Americans are criminally-minded.
    D. it increases the number of people who participates in welfare.

7. Despite the fact that he received less than 10 percent of the African American vote, President George W. Bush appointed African Americans to high positions in his cabinet. Which of the following is a good example?
    A. Condoleeza Rice, National Security Advisor
    B. Colin Powell, Vice President
    C. Lani Guinier, Attorney General
    D. Rod Paige, Secretary of Agriculture

8. Just before the 2000 election, Florida Governor Jeb Bush helped his brother by
    A. changing the election date in Florida.
    B. purging the voting rolls of 94,000 supposed felons and illegal voters.
    C. moving some friends to Florida so that they could vote.
    D. raising $8 million from conservative organizations.

9. Marlon Riggs challenged notions of Blackness and race by doing films on
    A. African Americans and homosexuality
    B. White flight into the suburbs
    C. He did frank films on prison life
    D. He did films on Black upper-class life

10. After the 1970s affirmative action came under attack in several cases. Which of the following was NOT an affirmative action case?
    A. Hopwood v. University of Texas Law School
    B. Bakke v. University of California
    C. Gratz v. Bollinger
    D. White v. Clemmons

11. President Bill Clinton appointed John Hope Franklin to chair his
    A. Panel on Initiative on Race.
    B. Civil Rights Commission.
    C. Commission on Women in Higher Education.
    D. Commission on Minority Rights.

12. Louis Farrakhan called for a Million Man March on Washington to
    A. protest George Bush's veto of the 1990 Civil Rights Act.
    B. protest high incarceration rates amongst African American males.
    C. have a day of national atonement for Black males.
    D. protest the unfair drug laws and sentencing practices.

13.   During the 1990s Angela Davis gained national fame by protesting against the
            A. high rates of poverty in the northeast.
            B. high rates of incarceration amongst African Americans.
            C. low voter turnouts in national elections by African Americans.
            D. lack of Black jurors on trials involving African American defendants.

14.   Johnnie Cochran gained international fame for his defense of O.J. Simpson. Before the
        Simpson trial, what was Cochran known for?
            A. He was one of the best product liability lawyers in the west.
            B. He was the first Black judge elected in Los Angeles County.
            C. He had successfully sued the Los Angeles Police Department for abusing
               suspects.
            D. He had prosecuted some of the most famous criminals in California.

15.   President Clinton worked with the Republicans to "end Welfare as we know it." What
        was the bill he signed to change welfare?
            A. The Welfare Responsibility Act
            B. The Welfare to Work Act
            C. The Personal Responsibility and Work Opportunity Reconciliation Act
            D. The Welfare Reform Act

THOUGHT QUESTIONS

1. What was President Clinton trying to say by having Maya Angelou deliver a poem before his inauguration?

2. What did reactions to the videotaped beatings of Rodney King reveal about the perspectives of black and white Americans regarding race?

3. Why was welfare reform considered such a controversial issue for African Americans?

4. Johnnie Cochran clearly played upon the prevailing racial opinions of America. How did the Simpson case uncover the racial differences between Blacks and Whites?

5. Discuss the ways that the prison system has been used to undermine the gains made by African Americans.

ANSWER KEY MULTIPLE CHOICE QUESTIONS

1. D
2. B
3. C
4. C
5. A
6. D
7. A
8. B
9. A
10. D
11. A
12. C
13. B
14. C
15. C